Better Homes and Gardens

CHRISTMAS
FROM THE HEART

Volume 23

Elizabeth M. Burd
2016

Meredith Consumer Marketing
Des Moines, Iowa

CHRISTMAS
FROM THE HEART

MEREDITH CORPORATION CONSUMER MARKETING
Vice President, Consumer Marketing: Janet Donnelly
Consumer Marketing Product Director: Heather Sorensen
Consumer Marketing Product Manager: Mary Ripperger
Business Director: Ron Clingman
Senior Production Manager: Al Rodruck
Photographers: Jay Wilde, Marty Baldwin, Jason Donnelly

WATERBURY PUBLICATIONS, INC.
Contributing Editor: Carol Field Dahlstrom
Contributing Food Stylist: Jennifer Peterson
Contributing Copy Editor: Terri Fredrickson
Contributing Proofreader: Linda Wagner

Editorial Director: Lisa Kingsley
Creative Director: Ken Carlson
Associate Editors: Tricia Bergman, Mary Williams
Associate Design Director: Doug Samuelson
Production Assistant: Mindy Samuelson

BETTER HOMES AND GARDENS® MAGAZINE
Editor in Chief: Gayle Goodson Butler
Art Director: Michael D. Belknap
Senior Deputy Editor: Nancy Wall Hopkins
Editorial Assistant: Renee Irey

MEREDITH PUBLISHING GROUP
President: Tom Harty

MEREDITH CORPORATION
Chairman and Chief Executive Officer: Stephen M. Lacy

In Memoriam: E.T. Meredith III (1933–2003)

Contents

HAVE THE BEST HOLIDAY EVER!

Christmastime is your favorite time of year! (It is our favorite time too!) You love to get out your treasured ornaments, put up a stunning tree, and surround yourself with family and friends. You stay up late to wrap your beautiful packages and you can't wait to make your own clever greeting cards. Your kitchen is filled with the aroma of the holidays as you bake dozens of Christmas cookies.

Creating your own handmade Christmas is one of the joys of the season. And in this book you'll find page after page of projects, ideas, and recipes to make this holiday one to remember. You'll find felt ornaments to embroider and table runners to quilt. There are vellum paper trees to craft and nature-inspired wraps for those special gifts. You'll find a snowman hat to crochet and colorful pillows to stitch. You'll even find quick and easy centerpieces to make just in the nick of time. Gifts from the kitchen are always favorites! You'll find an entire chapter of ideas for making and packaging those tempting treats.

So make this the best holiday ever by filling your home with a handmade Christmas and making memories that will last forever—a Christmas from the Heart.

The editors

Fruits of the Season

You'll be dreaming of sugarplums this Christmas
season while you decorate your holiday home with
the luscious shapes and rich colors of naturally
beautiful fruits and berries.

PLUM

PEACH

STRAWBERRY

POMEGRANATE

Embroidered Felt Fruit Trims

The soft and rich colors of nonwoven felt make the perfect material to craft a set of trims for your Christmas tree. Add sparkling sequins and simple embroidery stitches to embellish these heirloom-quality pieces.

WHAT YOU NEED
For All of the Fruit Trims:
Tracing paper • Pencil • Scissors • Embroidery needle • Gold-green sequins • Gold seed beads • Fine needle for beads and sequins • Polyester fibertill • Narrow metallic gold ribbon for hanging • Nonwoven felt such as National Nonwovens • Embroidery floss

For the Peach: National Nonwovens felt:
Georgia Peach 2820, Pea Soup 0729
Embroidery floss: DMC #350, #814, #435

For the Pear: National Nonwovens felt:
Native Maize 0437, Lemon Lime 2113, Pea Soup 0729
Embroidery floss: DMC #814, #921, #731

For the Plum: National Nonwovens felt:
Grape Jelly 2349, Lemon Lime 2113, Hydrangea 2345
Embroidery floss: DMC #554, #435, #3820, #731

For the Apple: National Nonwovens felt:
Strawberry Parfait 2201, Native Maize 0437,
Pea Soup 0729, Pistachio 0703
Embroidery floss: DMC #3820, #554, #166, #731

For the Strawberry: National Nonwovens felt:
Ruby Red Slipper 2212, Pistachio 0703
Embroidery floss: DMC #350, #554, #731

For the Pomegranate: National Nonwovens felt:
Burnt Sienna 2206, Deep Red 2201, Native Maize 0437
Embroidery floss: DMC #921, #731

WHAT YOU DO
For All Fruits
1. Copy and trace the patterns, pages 12–14, and cut out. Draw around the patterns onto the suggested color of felt. Cut out.
2. Embroider the small circles on each fruit piece, referring to the photos for the stitches used. (For Stitch Diagrams, see page 160.) Add sequins as desired to the small circles. For the Strawberry, fold the circles and embellish at fold as indicated on the pattern. Embroider leaves and add sequins or French knots and set aside.
3. Using the whip stitch, for all of the fruits except the strawberry, sew the two larger main fruit shapes together, starting at the bottom and sewing the leaves in the seam while stitching. Leave an opening at the bottom (but leave the needle on the thread) and lightly stuff the piece.
4. Use the running stitch to attach the small circle onto the large fruit shape starting at the bottom and sewing up to the top and back down going through all of the layers.
5. Finish sewing the large fruit piece together, hiding the thread from attaching the smaller piece inside. Add hanging loop at top, tucking the loop inside the two stuffed pieces. Secure thread at ends.
6. For the strawberry, embellish front of strawberry with sequins and French knots, attaching the sequins with French knots. Use the running stitch to sew the two main pieces together leaving an opening for stuffing at the top. Stuff lightly and sew shut. Sew folded leaves at top.
7. For all other fruits, tack embellished leaves in place, referring to photos for placement.

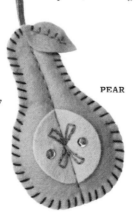

PEAR

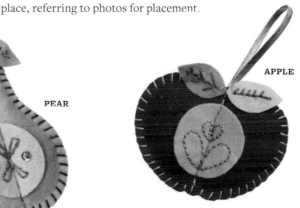

APPLE

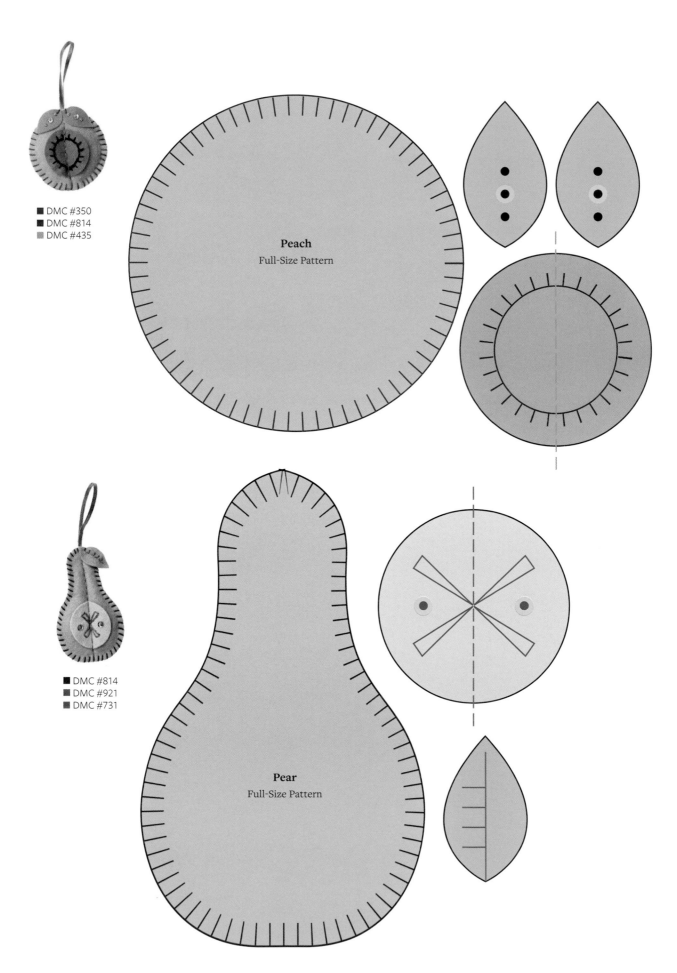

DMC #350
DMC #814
DMC #435

Peach
Full-Size Pattern

DMC #814
DMC #921
DMC #731

Pear
Full-Size Pattern

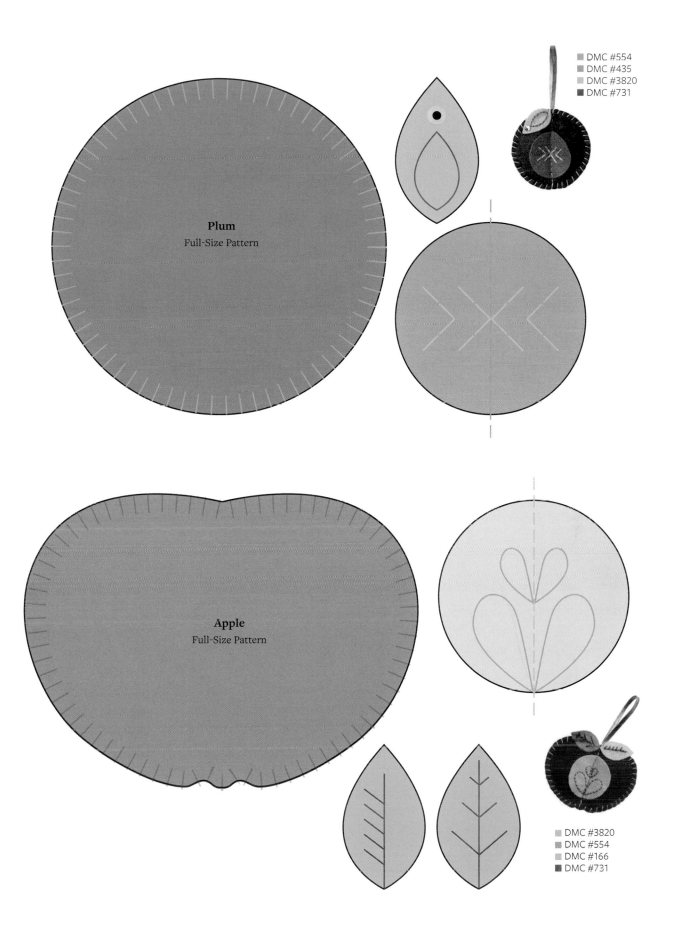

Plum
Full-Size Pattern

■ DMC #554
■ DMC #435
■ DMC #3820
■ DMC #731

Apple
Full-Size Pattern

■ DMC #3820
■ DMC #554
■ DMC #166
■ DMC #731

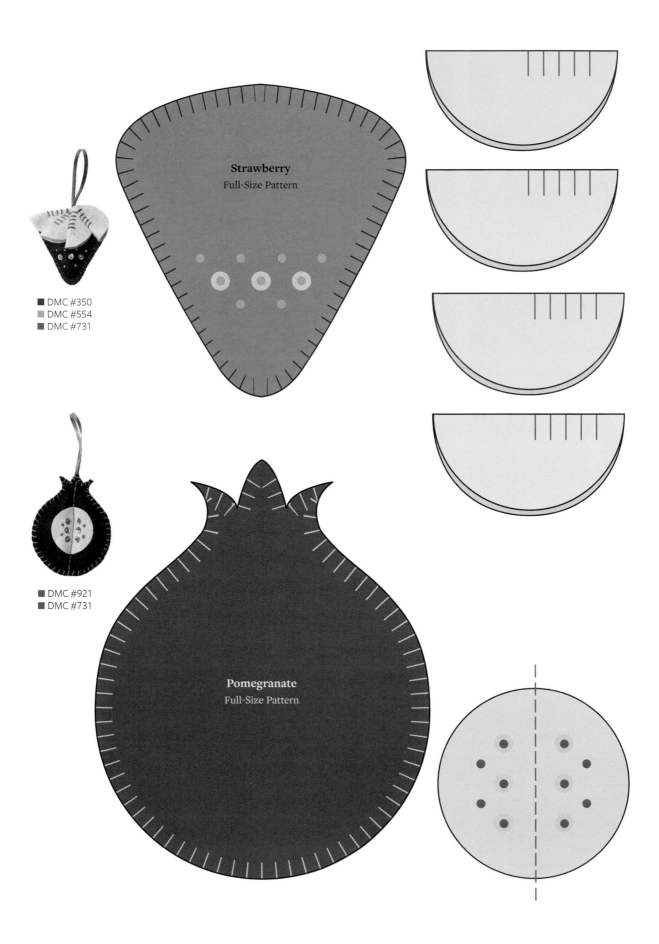

Strawberry
Full-Size Pattern

■ DMC #350
■ DMC #554
■ DMC #731

■ DMC #921
■ DMC #731

Pomegranate
Full-Size Pattern

A vintage mirror becomes a pretty piece of holiday decor when it is embellished with greenery and clusters of fruit.

Fruited Reflection

Reflect the beauty of the season by transforming a favorite mirror into a holiday piece of art.

WHAT YOU NEED

Mirror with wood edge • Real or artificial greenery • Artificial fruits such as pears, grapes, and berries • Hot-glue gun and hot glue

WHAT YOU DO

1. Be sure the mirror is clean and dry. Use hot glue to glue the greenery to the mirror. Real greenery will work but will not stay secure as long as artificial greenery.

2. Fill in one corner of the mirror by clustering the fruits atop the greenery. Let glue dry.

Sugarplum Fairy Centerpiece

A little dusting of sugar on beautiful fresh fruits and berries will give a soft and magical glow to your holiday centerpiece.

WHAT YOU NEED

Fresh fruit such as pears, plums, star fruits, small apples, cranberries, grapes, peaches, oranges, kumquats, or desired fruits • Fresh rosemary • Cookie sheet • Parchment paper • Powdered egg whites such as Deb El Just Whites • ½-inch paintbrush • Small dish • Fine sugar • Skewers • Small bowl • Cake plate

WHAT YOU DO

1. Be sure the fruit and rosemary are clean and dry. Lay the dry fruit and herbs on a parchment-covered cookie sheet.
2. Mix the powdered egg whites as specified on the manufacturer's label. Use the paintbrush to lightly paint each fruit. Immediately sprinkle with fine sugar. Skewer the small fruits and place in a glass or poke into an orange. For large fruits, work on one side at a time, letting one side dry before sugaring the other side.
3. For the rosemary, dip the rosemary into the egg-white mixture, shaking off any excess. Dust with sugar. Lay on parchment paper to dry.
4. After all pieces are dry, carefully arrange on cake plate tucking the sugared rosemary into the centerpiece.

Fruits of the Season Appliqué

Silk and cotton-blend fabrics are appliquéd into an elegant fruit-inspired table piece that becomes a treasured work of art.

WHAT YOU NEED

Final Dimensions: 16×20 inches
Fabric suggestions: 40 inches wide

For the Fabrics:
For the Background: ½ yard burlap-color cotton or silk fabric.
For the Appliqué: One fat quarter each assorted silk/cotton blend or cotton fabric in fruit colors for green and purple grapes, pineapple, and pineapple tops • One fat quarter each or large scraps assorted fruit color cotton batik or cotton print in fruit colors for orange, lime, apples, pears, and kumquats
For the Backing and Binding: ¾ yard coordinating cotton batik or cotton print (for backing and binding)

1 yard paper-backed fusible web
18×22-inch piece of quilt batting

WHAT YOU DO

Cut the Quilt Pieces
1. From the background fabric cut an 18×22-inch rectangle.
2. From the backing fabric cut three 2¼-inch strips for binding. Cut an 18×22-inch rectangle for backing.

Prepare the Appliqué Pieces
1. Trace the fruit pattern pieces, pages 20–22, onto the paper side of paper-backed fusible web, tracing the number of times indicated on the pattern. (The patterns are the reverse of the finished design.) Mark the pineapple leaf pattern numbers near one edge.
2. Cut around the pattern pieces ¼ inch outside the traced lines. If desired, remove the fusible web from the center of the pattern pieces by cutting ¼ inch inside the traced line. This will give the finished appliqué a softer feel.
3. Referring to the paper-backed fusible web directions, fuse the patterns to the wrong side of the appropriate fabrics. Cut out on the traced lines.

Arrange the Appliqué
1. Remove paper backing from the pineapple leaves and arrange in numerical order on a nonstick pressing sheet, overlapping as indicated. In the same manner fuse together the three lady apples and the orange wedge.
2. Remove paper backing and arrange the other fruit and the fused pieces to the background rectangle referring to the Appliqué Layout, page 22, or as desired. Fruit should be positioned 2 to 2½ inches from the edge of the background. Fuse in place.

Stitch the Appliqué
1. Layer the quilt top, batting, and backing.
2. Using a matching color stitch around each pattern piece with a small zigzag stitch (about 1.5 mm wide and 1 mm long) or a narrow satin zigzag stitch.
3. Quilt as desired in the apples, pears, oranges, and kumquats. For the pineapple texture stitch diagonal lines about 1 inch apart. For the grapes stitch oval circles. Stitch veins in the grape leaves. Mark the grape tendril and stitch using a 2.5-mm-wide satin zigzag stitch.
4. Quilt the background as desired.

Finish the Quilt
1. Trim the top to 16×20 inches straightening the edges and squaring the corners. Fruit should be about 1½ inches from the bottom edge.
2. Join together the binding strips with diagonal seams to make a continuous strip. Use to bind the quilt.
3. For added detail, stitch an accent line of stitching in the ditch of the binding. Use a triple stitch and two colors of purple thread. Using two strands of embroidery floss, make a French knot in the center of each pineapple square.

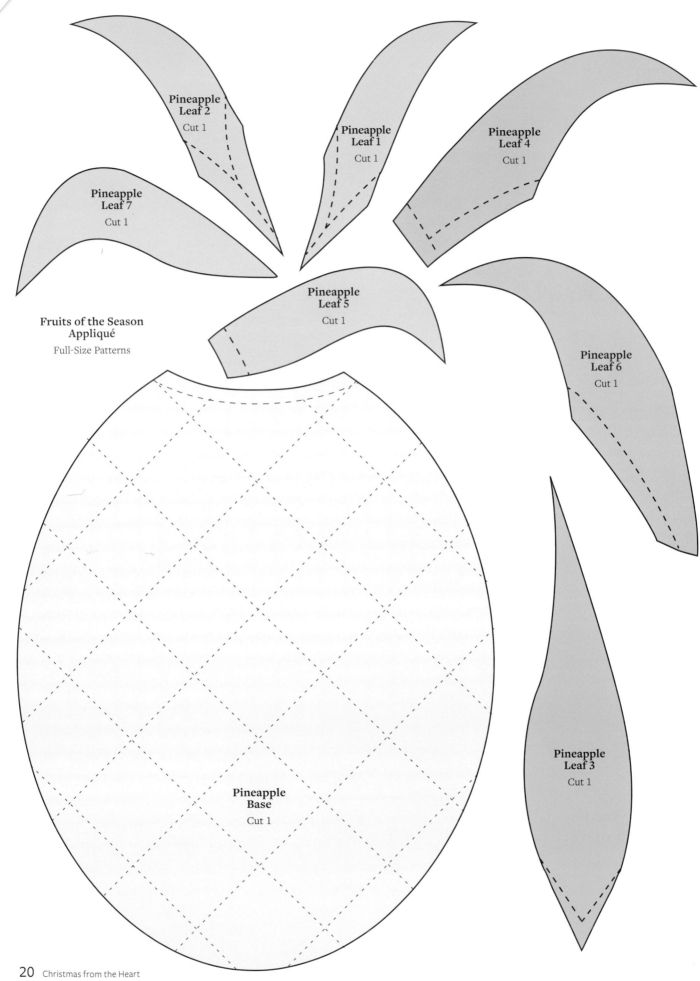

Pineapple Leaf 2
Cut 1

Pineapple Leaf 1
Cut 1

Pineapple Leaf 4
Cut 1

Pineapple Leaf 7
Cut 1

Fruits of the Season Appliqué
Full-Size Patterns

Pineapple Leaf 5
Cut 1

Pineapple Leaf 6
Cut 1

Pineapple Base
Cut 1

Pineapple Leaf 3
Cut 1

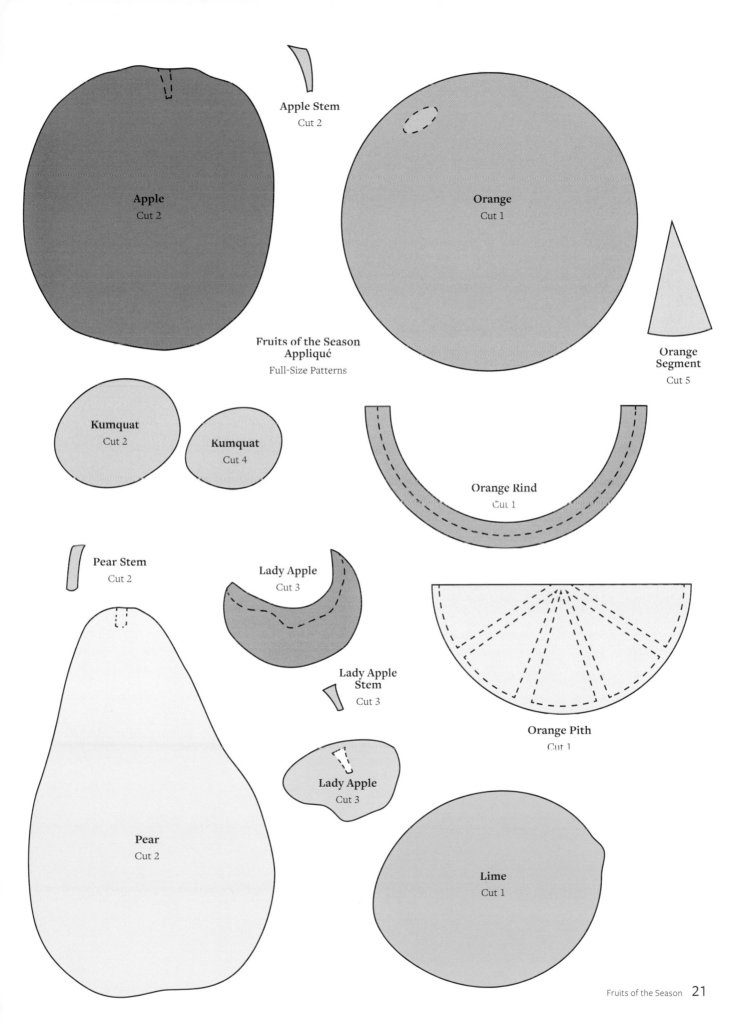

Apple Stem
Cut 2

Apple
Cut 2

Orange
Cut 1

Fruits of the Season
Appliqué
Full-Size Patterns

Orange
Segment
Cut 5

Kumquat
Cut 2

Kumquat
Cut 4

Orange Rind
Cut 1

Pear Stem
Cut 2

Lady Apple
Cut 3

Lady Apple
Stem
Cut 3

Orange Pith
Cut 1

Lady Apple
Cut 3

Pear
Cut 2

Lime
Cut 1

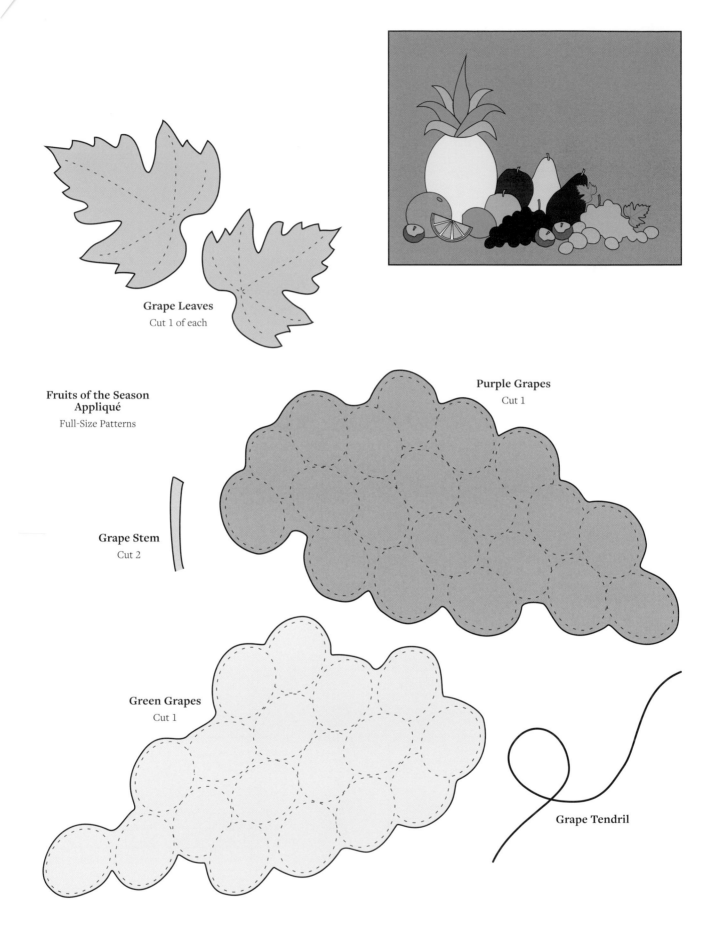

Grape Leaves
Cut 1 of each

Fruits of the Season Appliqué

Full-Size Patterns

Grape Stem
Cut 2

Purple Grapes
Cut 1

Green Grapes
Cut 1

Grape Tendril

Golden Fruit Table Setting

Set your table with the colors of your favorite fruits—rich kumquat golds, cranberry reds, and soft pear greens.

WHAT YOU NEED
2½×6-inch piece of brown kraft paper • 3×7-inch piece of cranberry-color cardstock • Purchased large initial stickers • Scissors • Crafts glue • Transparent tape (optional) • Pinking shears • Gold or white dishes • Gold, light lime green, or white napkin • Purchased acrylic grapes • Small piece of greenery • Small vintage ornament

WHAT YOU DO
1. To make the napkin ring, trim the brown kraft paper using the pinking shears. Adhere to the cranberry-color cardstock using crafts glue. Attach the initial in the center of the napkin ring. Bend the paper around the napkin and secure with tape or crafts glue.
2. Layer the dishes on the table cloth. Tuck grapes, greenery, and a vintage ornament beside the napkin.

Christmas Morning Brunch

If the promise of stuffed stockings doesn't rouse sleepyheads from their beds, surely the smells of a yummy brunch will. And as a gift for the cook, everything can be prepped or made ahead.

Four-Cheese Zucchini Strata

Strata simply means "layers." This dish features luscious layers of garlic focaccia, sauteed zucchini, and four cheeses.

WHAT YOU NEED

2 tablespoons olive oil
4 medium zucchini, halved lengthwise and cut into ¼-inch slices (about 5 cups)
  Butter
8 cups bite-size pieces Italian flatbread with garlic (focaccia)
1 cup shredded provolone cheese (4 ounces)
1 cup shredded white cheddar cheese (4 ounces)
½ cup crumbled blue cheese (2 ounces)
½ cup grated Parmesan cheese (2 ounces)
7 eggs, lightly beaten
2 cups milk
2 tablespoons snipped fresh parsley
½ teaspoon salt
½ teaspoon ground black pepper

WHAT YOU DO

1. In a very large skillet heat olive oil over medium-high heat. Gradually add zucchini slices. Cook until zucchini is lightly browned, stirring occasionally. Remove from heat. Meanwhile, lightly butter a 3-quart rectangular or oval baking dish. Place half of the torn bread in the prepared dish. Arrange half of the zucchini over the bread. Sprinkle half of each cheese over the zucchini. Repeat layers.
2. In a large bowl whisk together eggs, milk, parsley, salt, and pepper. Pour evenly over layers in baking dish. Cover with plastic wrap. Chill for at least 2 hours or up to 24 hours.
3. Preheat oven to 325°F. Remove plastic wrap. Bake for 45 to 50 minutes or until center is set and an instant-read thermometer inserted into the center registers 170°F. Let stand for 10 minutes before serving. Makes 8 to 10 servings.

Sugared Bacon-Wrapped Sausages

Applewood-smoked bacon and a dash of spice update this classic morning side.

WHAT YOU NEED

  Nonstick cooking spray
24 small cooked smoked sausage links
8 slices applewood-smoked bacon or plain bacon, each slice cut crosswise into thirds
⅓ cup packed brown sugar
½ teaspoon Chinese five-spice powder or apple pie spice

WHAT YOU DO

1. Preheat oven to 300°F. Line a 15×10×1-inch baking pan with foil; lightly coat with cooking spray. Set aside.
2. Wrap each sausage link with a bacon piece, overlapping the bacon piece at the end. Press the end of the bacon piece to seal or secure it with a wooden toothpick.
3. In a large resealable plastic bag combine brown sugar and five-spice powder. Add several bacon-wrapped sausages to bag; seal. Shake bag gently to coat sausages with brown sugar mixture; place sausages in prepared pan. Repeat with remaining bacon-wrapped sausages and brown sugar mixture.
4. Bake for 1 hour or until the bacon browns. Serve immediately. Makes 24 sausages.
To Make Ahead: Start with Step 2. Cover and chill for up to 24 hours. To serve, prepare Step 1, then continue as directed in Step 3.

Mascarpone-Stuffed French Toast with Salted Caramel-Banana Sauce

A celebratory holiday brunch is the perfect time to indulge in this rich and decadent treat. Just a little bit of sea salt in the caramel sauce heightens the flavor.

WHAT YOU NEED

12 slices Texas toast
1 8-ounce package cream cheese, softened
½ cup mascarpone cheese (4 ounces)
½ cup chopped pecans or macadamia nuts, toasted
2 tablespoons packed brown sugar
1 teaspoon ground cinnamon
¼ teaspoon salt
6 eggs, lightly beaten
3 cups milk
¼ teaspoon salt
1 recipe Salted Caramel-Banana Sauce
  Chopped pecans or macadamia nuts, toasted (optional)

WHAT YOU DO

1. Arrange half of the bread slices in a single layer in a 3-quart rectangular baking dish. In a small bowl combine cream cheese, mascarpone cheese, pecans, brown sugar, cinnamon, and salt. Spread cheese mixture evenly over bread in baking dish. Top with the remaining bread slices to make six stacks.

2. In a medium bowl whisk together eggs, milk, and salt. Pour egg mixture evenly over bread stacks, covering all of the tops. Cover with plastic wrap. Chill for at least 2 hours or up to 24 hours.

3. Preheat oven to 375°F. Line a 15×10×1-inch baking pan with parchment paper. Arrange bread stacks in the prepared pan. Bake about 1 hour or until golden, turning stacks every 15 minutes. Serve warm with Salted Caramel-Banana Sauce. Sprinkle with additional toasted pecans or macadamia nuts, if desired. Makes 12 servings.

Salted Caramel-Banana Sauce: In a heavy medium saucepan stir together ¾ cup packed brown sugar, ½ cup whipping cream, ½ cup butter, and 2 tablespoons light-color corn syrup. Bring to boiling over medium-high heat, whisking occasionally; reduce heat to medium. Boil gently for 3 minutes more. Remove from heat. Stir in 1 teaspoon vanilla and ½ teaspoon sea salt. Pour into a small bowl. Cool to room temperature. If desired, cover and chill for up to 24 hours. (If chilled, let stand at room temperature for 1 hour before serving.) Stir in 1 banana, thinly sliced.

This indulgent stuffed French toast looks and tastes like it was ordered off the menu at a fancy restaurant, but it is very simple to make—and it can chill in the refrigerator for up to 24 hours before baking.

Danish Fruit and Cheese Rolls

These bakery-quality Danish pastries start with frozen sweet roll dough, so they go together in a snap.

WHAT YOU NEED

2   16-ounce loaves frozen sweet roll dough, thawed
1   3-ounce package cream cheese, softened
1   egg yolk
2   tablespoons sugar
1   tablespoon all-purpose flour
¼   teaspoon vanilla
¼   teaspoon almond extract or finely shredded orange peel
¼   cup desired-flavor jam, preserves, canned pie filling, or fruit curd

WHAT YOU DO

1. Line two large baking sheets with parchment paper; set aside.

2. To shape spiral pastries, on a lightly floured surface roll one loaf of dough into a 12-inch square. Cut square into twelve 12×1-inch strips. With one end of a strip in each hand, twist ends in opposite directions three or four times. Coil the strip into a spiral round, tucking the outside end underneath. Repeat with remaining strips, placing 2 inches apart on baking sheets. Repeat with the remaining loaf of sweet roll dough. Cover and let rise in a warm place until nearly double in size (30 to 45 minutes). Meanwhile, in a small bowl combine cream cheese, egg yolk, sugar, flour, vanilla, and almond extract. Beat with an electric mixer on medium speed until well mixed and smooth. Preheat oven to 350°F. Spoon a rounded measuring teaspoon of the cream cheese mixture into the center of each coil.

3. Bake for 15 to 18 minutes or until golden. Cool pastries slightly on a wire rack. Top the center of each pastry coil with ½ teaspoon jam. Serve warm or at room temperature. Makes 24 pastries.

Turnovers: On a lightly floured surface roll one loaf of dough into a 12×9-inch rectangle. Cut rectangle into twelve 3-inch squares. Place a rounded measuring teaspoon of cream cheese mixture into the center of each square. Top each with ½ teaspoon jam. Fold each pastry square diagonally in half. Using the tines of a fork, seal edges. With fork, poke a few holes in the top of each triangle. Place on prepared baking sheets. Cover and let rise in a warm place until nearly double in size (30 to 45 minutes). Repeat with the remaining loaf of sweet roll dough, remaining cream cheese mixture, and remaining jam. Bake as directed in Step 3. If desired, drizzle with Lemon Curd Icing. Serve warm or at room temperature. Makes 24 pastries.

Lemon Curd Icing: In a small bowl combine ¾ cup powdered sugar, 1 tablespoon lemon curd, ¼ teaspoon vanilla, and, if desired, ⅛ teaspoon almond extract. Stir in 1 tablespoon milk. If necessary, add additional milk, 1 teaspoon at a time, to reach drizzling consistency.

Envelopes: On a lightly floured surface roll one loaf of dough into a 12×9-inch rectangle. Cut rectangle into twelve 3-inch squares. Place a rounded measuring teaspoon of cream cheese mixture into the center of each square. Top each with ½ teaspoon jam. Fold points to the center, forming an envelope. Pinch points together in the center to seal. (If necessary to seal, lightly moisten points with water.) Cover and let rise in a warm place until nearly double in size (30 to 45 minutes). Repeat with the remaining loaf of sweet roll dough, remaining cream cheese mixture, and remaining jam. Bake as directed in Step 3. Serve warm or at room temperature. Makes 24 pastries.

To Make Ahead: Prepare as directed through Step 2, except do not top with cream cheese mixture. Cover and chill rolls and cream cheese mixture separately for up to 24 hours. To serve, preheat oven to 350°F. Top rolls with cream cheese mixture. Continue as directed.

Store-bought Danish pastries often feature either fruit filling or cream cheese. These beauties are filled with both, so you don't have to choose!

Pear-Brie Strudel Rolls

You must plan ahead to make these buttery fruit-and-cheese rolls. The phyllo dough needs to thaw about 24 hours in the refrigerator before using.

WHAT YOU NEED

- 1½ cups chopped pears (1½ medium)
- 1 cup apple juice or water
- 3 tablespoons maple syrup
- ¼ to ½ teaspoon snipped fresh thyme (optional)
- ½ cup finely chopped walnuts or chopped slivered almonds
- ⅓ cup dried cherries, snipped
- 2 tablespoons packed brown sugar
- ½ teaspoon apple pie spice
- 15 sheets frozen phyllo dough (14×9-inch rectangles), thawed
- ½ cup butter, melted
- 18 thin slices Brie cheese (4 ounces)
  Fresh thyme sprigs (optional)

WHAT YOU DO

1. Preheat oven to 400°F. Line a baking sheet with parchment paper or foil; set aside.

2. For filling, in a small saucepan combine pears, apple juice, maple syrup, and, if desired, snipped thyme. Bring to boiling; reduce heat. Simmer, uncovered, about 5 minutes or until pears are tender. Drain pears; discard liquid. Return pears to saucepan. Add nuts and cherries to saucepan. Add brown sugar and apple pie spice; toss gently until mixed. Set aside.

3. Unroll phyllo dough. Stack five phyllo sheets on a work surface, brushing each sheet lightly with some of the melted butter before topping with the next. Cut phyllo stack lengthwise in half and crosswise in thirds to form six squares.

4. Place a slice of Brie cheese near the bottom edge of a phyllo square. Spoon 1 rounded tablespoon of filling on top. Fold bottom edge over filling; fold in sides. Roll up around filling. Place on prepared baking sheet. Repeat with remaining phyllo sheets, melted butter, Brie, and pear mixture to form 12 more rolls. Brush tops with some of the remaining melted butter.

5. Bake for 13 to 15 minutes or until rolls are golden. (Rolls may leak slightly during baking.) Cool on a wire rack. Serve slightly warm. If desired, garnish with fresh thyme. Makes 18 rolls.

To Make Ahead: Prepare as directed through Step 4, except do not preheat oven. Place baking sheet in the freezer and freeze until firm. Place rolls in a freezer container. Seal, label, and freeze for up to 3 months. To serve, preheat oven to 400°F. Line a baking sheet with parchment paper or foil. Place frozen rolls on prepared baking sheet. Bake for 18 to 20 minutes or until rolls are golden.

Gingerbread-Sour Cream Muffins

The sour cream in these warmly spiced muffins makes them terrifically tender. They are best served right out of the oven. (Pictured on page 25)

WHAT YOU NEED

- 2 cups unbleached all-purpose flour or all-purpose flour
- 1 tablespoon finely chopped fresh ginger or 1 teaspoon ground ginger
- 2 teaspoons baking powder
- ¾ teaspoon ground allspice or cinnamon
- ¼ teaspoon baking soda
- ¼ teaspoon salt
- ¼ cup butter
- 1 egg, lightly beaten
- 1 8-ounce carton sour cream
- ⅓ cup milk
- ¼ cup packed brown sugar
- ¼ cup mild-flavor molasses
- 2 tablespoons granulated sugar
- 2 tablespoons finely snipped crystallized ginger

WHAT YOU DO

1. Preheat oven to 400°F. Grease the bottoms of twelve 2½-inch muffin cups; set aside.

2. In a medium bowl stir together flour, fresh or ground ginger, baking powder, allspice, baking soda, and salt. Using a pastry blender, cut in butter until mixture resembles coarse crumbs. Make a well in center of flour mixture.

3. In another medium bowl combine egg, sour cream, milk, brown sugar, and molasses. Add egg mixture all at once to flour mixture. Stir just until moistened (batter should be lumpy). Spoon batter into the prepared cups, filling each nearly full.

4. In a small bowl combine granulated sugar and crystallized ginger. Sprinkle over muffin batter.

5. Bake for 18 to 20 minutes or until golden brown and a toothpick inserted near the centers comes out clean. Cool in pan on a wire rack for 5 minutes. Remove from pan; serve warm. Makes 12 muffins.

To Make Ahead: Place baked and completely cooled muffins in a single layer in an airtight container; seal. Freeze for up to 1 month. To serve, thaw at room temperature. To reheat, wrap muffins in foil. Heat in a 350°F oven for 12 to 15 minutes or until warm.

Cranberry-Chocolate Scones

For the most tender-textured scones, work the dough as little as possible when kneading it in Step 3. (Pictured on page 24)

WHAT YOU NEED

2½ cups all-purpose flour
2   tablespoons sugar
1   tablespoon baking powder
¼   teaspoon salt
⅓   cup butter
2   eggs, lightly beaten
¾   cup whipping cream
¼   cup chopped dried cranberries
¼   cup miniature semisweet chocolate pieces
½   teaspoon finely shredded orange peel (optional)
    Whipping cream or milk
1   recipe Orange Drizzle

WHAT YOU DO

1. Preheat oven to 400°F. In a large bowl combine flour, sugar, baking powder, and salt. Using a pastry blender, cut in butter until mixture resembles coarse crumbs. Make a well in the center of the flour mixture; set aside.
2. In a medium bowl combine eggs, the ¾ cup cream, the cranberries, chocolate pieces, and, if desired, orange peel. Add egg mixture all at once to flour mixture. Using a fork, stir just until mixture is moistened.
3. Turn dough out onto a lightly floured surface. Knead dough by folding and gently pressing for 10 to 12 strokes or until dough is nearly smooth. Divide dough in half. Pat or lightly roll each portion into a 6-inch circle. Cut each circle into six wedges.
4. Place wedges 2 inches apart on an ungreased baking sheet. Brush wedges with additional cream. Bake for 12 to 14 minutes or until golden. Cool slightly on baking sheet. Drizzle with Orange Drizzle. Serve warm or at room temperature. Makes 12 scones.

Orange Drizzle: In a bowl combine 1 cup powdered sugar, 1 tablespoon orange juice, and ¼ teaspoon vanilla. Stir in additional orange juice, 1 teaspoon at a time, to reach drizzling consistency.

To Make Ahead: Prepare as directed, except do not drizzle with Orange Drizzle. Place cooled scones in a resealable plastic freezer bag. Seal, label, and freeze for up to 2 months. To serve, thaw at room temperature. If desired, preheat oven to 350°F. Place scones on a baking sheet; heat for 8 to 10 minutes. Drizzle with Orange Drizzle.

Eggnog Trifles

The eggnog custard, made with gelatin—similar to panna cotta—requires no cooking and sets up after chilling.

WHAT YOU NEED

For the Eggnog Custard:
1   7.2-gram envelope unflavored gelatin
3   tablespoons water
2½ cups whipping cream
1   cup eggnog
⅔   cup sugar
    Large pinch salt
¼   teaspoon freshly grated nutmeg

For the Filling Layers:
¾   cup strawberry or raspberry jam
2   teaspoons lemon juice
    Purchased or homemade star cookies sprinkled with sugar and nutmeg (optional)

WHAT YOU DO

For the Eggnog Custard:
1. In a small bowl stir together gelatin and the water. Let stand for 5 minutes.
2. Meanwhile, in a medium saucepan combine cream, eggnog, sugar, and salt. Heat over medium heat, stirring occasionally, until hot. Remove from heat. Stir in gelatin. Cool slightly for about 10 minutes, stirring occasionally. (Stirring prevents the gelatin from sinking to the bottom.) Immediately pour custard into dishes as directed in Layer 1.

For the Trifle Assembly
Layer 1: Divide Eggnog Custard among ten 6-ounce coffee cups or other dishes. Loosely cover with plastic wrap. Refrigerate about 2 hours, until set.
Layer 2: Sprinkle nutmeg on custard.
Layer 3: In a small bowl whisk together jam and lemon juice. Spoon into each cup, spreading to cover custard. Refrigerate 2 hours or overnight.
Layer 4: To serve, top each trifle with a sugar cookie, if desired. Makes 10 servings.

Berry Cheesecake Parfaits

These pretty parfaits taste like cheesecake—but with no baking required! Instead, Brie and cream cheese combine to simulate the flavors.

WHAT YOU NEED

- 1   5-ounce package creamy-style Brie, softened, or Brie cheese, rind removed
- 11 ounces cream cheese, softened (use one 8-ounce package and one 3-ounce package)
- ⅓   to ½ cup sugar
- 1   tablespoon lemon juice
     Kosher salt
- 6   cups sliced fresh strawberries, blueberries, raspberries, and/or mixed cut-up fruit
- ¼   cup butter toffee-glazed sliced almonds
     Honey (optional)

WHAT YOU DO

1. In a medium bowl beat Brie, cream cheese, sugar, lemon juice, and a pinch of salt with an electric mixer on medium speed until smooth. Set aside.

2. Layer fruit and cheese mixture in eight parfait glasses or water goblets. Top with almonds. If desired, drizzle with honey. Makes 8 parfaits.

To Make Ahead: If you wish to make Berry Cheesecake Parfaits ahead, do not use apples, pears, or peaches because the fruit will turn brown. Prepare the cheese mixture and fruit as directed. Place cheese mixture and fruit in separate airtight containers. Cover and chill for up to 24 hours. To serve, let cheese mixture stand at room temperature for 30 minutes. Assemble as directed. (Or prepare parfaits as directed. Cover and chill the finished parfaits for up to 4 hours.)

Mulled Cranberry Punch

For a spicy-sweet garnish, line the rims of each glass with cinnamon sugar.

WHAT YOU NEED

- 1   orange
- 8   inches stick cinnamon, broken
- 8   whole cloves
- 4   whole allspice
- 4   cups water
- 1   32-ounce bottle cranberry juice
- 1   11.5-ounce can frozen white grape-raspberry juice concentrate
     Strips of orange peel (optional)

WHAT YOU DO

1. Use a vegetable peeler to remove several 2- to 3-inch-long sections of orange peel from the orange, avoiding the white pith underneath. Juice the orange.

2. For a spice bag, cut a 6- to 8-inch square from a double thickness of 100-percent-cotton cheesecloth. Place orange peel, cinnamon, cloves, and allspice in center of cheesecloth square. Bring up the corners; tie closed with 100-percent-cotton kitchen string.

3. In a large bowl combine the water, cranberry juice, juice concentrate, orange juice, and spice bag.

4. Carefully pour juice mixture into a 3½- or 4-quart slow cooker. Cover; cook on low-heat setting for 4 to 6 hours or on high-heat setting for 2 to 2½ hours. Discard spice bag. Serve immediately or keep warm on low-heat setting for up to 2 hours. If desired, garnish each drink with a strip of orange peel. Makes 12 (6-ounce) servings.

To Make Ahead: Prepare through Step 3. Cover bowl and chill for up to 24 hours. To serve, continue as directed in Step 4.

Pump up the holiday spirit of your drinks with festive garnishes such as fresh rosemary sprigs, fresh or frozen cranberries, kumquats, pomegranate seeds, cinnamon sticks, red and green maraschino cherries, and mint leaves.

Winter Fruit Sangria

You'll love how the figs, apricots, cranberries, and raisins infuse the wine with soft, warm flavors. Serve the drink alongside additional dried fruit so guests can easily spot the subtle goodness of each fruit in the wine.

WHAT YOU NEED

6   dried Calimyrna (light) figs, sliced
6   dried apricots, cut into slivers
½ cup dried cranberries
½ cup raisins
¼ cup brandy
2   tablespoons honey
1   750-milliliter bottle Rioja or Merlot wine
1   10-ounce bottle club soda
    Ice cubes
    Fresh or frozen cranberries (optional)

WHAT YOU DO

1. In a medium saucepan stir together figs, apricots, cranberries, raisins, brandy, and honey. Cook over medium-low heat until simmering. Remove from heat; cool slightly. Add wine; stir. Chill for at least 4 hours or up to 24 hours.
2. To serve, strain wine mixture into a pitcher. Add club soda and ice cubes; stir gently. If desired, garnish with fresh or frozen cranberries. Makes 8 (about 4-ounce) servings.

Aztec Hot Chocolate

A slow cooker makes easy work of creating this hot chocolate, zipped up with a spicy hint of chipotle chile pepper.

WHAT YOU NEED

4   cups milk
2   cups half-and-half or whole milk
1   teaspoon instant espresso coffee powder
1   teaspoon ground cinnamon
½ teaspoon ground chipotle chile pepper
1½ cups semisweet chocolate pieces
    Sweetened whipped cream (optional)
    Ground cinnamon (optional)

WHAT YOU DO

1. In a large bowl combine milk, half-and-half, coffee powder, the 1 teaspoon cinnamon, and the ground chipotle chile pepper.
2. Transfer mixture to a 3½- or 4-quart slow cooker. Stir in chocolate pieces. Cover and cook on low-heat setting for 4 hours or on high-heat setting for 2 hours, vigorously whisking once halfway through cooking time. Serve immediately or keep warm on warm setting or low-heat setting for up to 2 hours.
3. Before serving, whisk well. To serve, ladle beverage into heatproof mugs or cups. If desired, garnish each serving with whipped cream and/or sprinkle with additional cinnamon. Makes 12 (4-ounce) servings.
To Make Ahead: Prepare through Step 1. Cover bowl and chill for up to 24 hours. To serve, continue as directed with Step 2.

Natural Impressions

Let nature inspire you with its glorious reds, rich browns, and lively greens as you plan your holiday decorating this year.

*Personalize your gifts
this year with a little
touch of nature and
a painted letter or
message. Choose
the colors you like to
coordinate with your
wrapped package.*

Tree Slice Package Topper

*Add a little bit of natural charm to your wrapped packages by
tying on a painted slice of wood from nature itself.*

WHAT YOU NEED

Branches (2- to 3-inch diameter) and table saw
or purchased wood slices • Drill • Letter stickers
• Painter's tape • Crafts paint in desired colors •
Paintbrush • Ribbon or string

WHAT YOU DO

1. Using a table saw, slice tree branches about ½ inch thick
or use purchased wood slices. **Note:** If cutting your own
wood slices, let the wood slices dry for at least two weeks
before painting.

2. Drill a small hole in the top of the wood slice in desired
size. Affix stickers and painter's tape to the wood slice and
paint to create the design. When paint is dry, remove
stickers and painter's tape. **Note:** Different stickers work
better than others. Test stickers and paint on a test slice
first. Attach to gift with ribbon or string.

Driftwood Coasters

A slice of driftwood becomes a much-used coaster when it holds a favorite cup of hot chocolate. Stack and tie them with twine for a quick and much-appreciated gift.

WHAT YOU NEED
Piece of driftwood at least 3 inches thick • Soft cloth • Band saw • Sandpaper • Twine

WHAT YOU DO
1. Use the band saw to cut the wood into 1½-inch pieces. Wipe the driftwood pieces with a soft cloth. Sand the edges slightly until smooth. Wipe again.
2. Stack the pieces and tie with the twine.

Seeded Mini Wreath

Tiny seeds are layered onto a mini wreath form to create a beautiful little wreath for your holiday tree.

WHAT YOU NEED
Sunflower seeds • Pumpkin seeds • Nature findings such as seed pods • Paper plates • 5-inch foam wreath form, such as Styrofoam • Fine gold string • Hot-glue gun and glue sticks

WHAT YOU DO
1. Organize the seeds and nature findings on paper plates. Tie the string around the top of the wreath form.
2. Place the wreath form on a table. Using hot glue, choose the desired seeds and arrange them, layering them while gluing in place. Let dry.

Naturally Stamped Wraps

Snippets of fresh greenery pressed into paint and then onto brown paper make lovely textured gift wrap for your favorite holiday presents.

WHAT YOU NEED

Brown kraft paper or plain-color wrapping paper • masking tape • Pieces of evergreen • Crafts paint in desired colors • Paintbrush • Paper plates • Waxed paper • White crafts glue (optional) • Glitter (optional) • Ribbon

WHAT YOU DO

1. Cut a section of brown kraft paper large enough to wrap the desired gift. Lay the paper on a large surface and tape each corner down to keep paper from moving around while you stamp it.
2. Lay the evergreen piece on a paper plate and paint with crafts paint. Gently press the paint-covered greenery onto gift wrap. **Tip:** To avoid getting your hands covered with the paint, lay a sheet of waxed paper over the leaf before pressing it onto the paper. To create different patterns, alternate colors of paint. Or use white crafts glue instead of paint. Make the design with the glue and dust with glitter. Let dry.
3. Finish the packages by tying with desired ribbon.

Let the texture of fresh greenery become the motif on your holiday packages this year. Choose a variety of paint colors and a dusting of glitter to make your packages sparkle. Then add some contrasting ribbons to finish your pretty wraps.

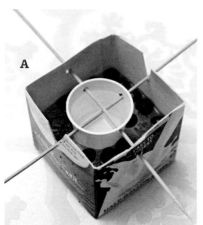

A

Icy Luminarias

Your guests will be amazed at your burning candles nestled into a beautiful block of cranberry-filled ice.

WHAT YOU NEED

Waxed milk carton • Scissors • Small paper cup • Paper punch • Wooden skewers • Water • Fresh cranberries, bits of orange slices, bits of fresh greenery • Votive candle • Plastic cup (for round block) • Large taper candle (for round block)

WHAT YOU DO

1. Cut the milk carton down to about 6 inches tall. Punch holes in two opposite sides about ½ inch from the top. Cut notches in the other two sides.

2. Fill the carton partially full with water. Add cranberries, orange pieces, and greenery.

3. Punch four holes, in sets of two across from each other, in the paper cup. Thread a skewer through the carton and then through two opposite holes in the cup. Thread the other skewer through the other two holes and set in the carton notches. See Photo A.

4. Fill the cup with water. Carefully set the carton outside if the temperature is below freezing or in the freezer. Freeze until firm.

5. To remove from carton, first remove the skewers and cup. Then run warm water over the bottom and around the cup. Set votive candle in ice and set on dish.

6. For round block variation, fill plastic cup with water, cranberries, and evergreen. Place large candle in center and freeze. Remove from freezer and light candle.

Never leave a burning candle unattended.

Nature offers a sweet little textured acorn cup to hold bright felt balls for a nature-inspired gift topper. They are easy to make and fun to use, so make these colorful gems by the dozens.

Acorn Package Toppers

Little felt beads are tucked into acorn tops to create charming little package toppers for your special gifts.

WHAT YOU NEED

Acorn tops • Purchased felt beads to fit into the tops
• Crafts glue • Natural color raffia

WHAT YOU DO

1. Be sure the acorn tops are clean and dry. Using a generous amount of crafts glue, glue the felt beads into the acorn tops. Let dry.
2. Wrap the package as desired. Wrap the raffia around the package. Glue the beads where the raffia intersects. Let dry.

Create holiday decorating pieces in no time when you use nature findings, fresh greenery, and purchased Christmas embellishments.

Nature Walk Frames

Pick up your favorite nature finds and adhere them along with bits of brown paper to the corner of a wood frame for a beautifully subtle look.

WHAT YOU NEED
Purchased wooden frames • Nature finds such as acorns and sticks • Crafts glue • Brown paper • Scissors

WHAT YOU DO
1. Cut holly shapes from the brown paper to fit the size of the frame. Glue the brown paper holly shapes at the corner of the frame.
2. Be sure the nature finds are clean and dry. Arrange the nature pieces and glue in place. Let dry.

Boxwood Topped Display

Use purchased assembled greenery to make quick work of creating a lovely Christmas container.

WHAT YOU NEED
Purchased square container • Dirt and moss • Fresh blue spruce twigs with pinecones • Purchased boxwood ball top • Wire • Purchased artificial dove

WHAT YOU DO
1. Fill the container with dirt and cover with moss. Insert the twigs and pinecones into the dirt.
2. Wrap a wire around the ball and insert into the dirt. Add the bird on top of the ball.

Winterberry Wreath

A starburst of winterberry stuck into a small block of florist's foam showcases a trio of decorative balls and adds brilliant flourish to a ready-made wreath.

WHAT YOU NEED
Small block of florist's foam • Purchased bay laurel wreath or other green wreath • Winterberry sprigs • Decorative balls on picks • Wire

WHAT YOU DO
1. Lay the florist's foam on a table and gently poke the winterberry into the foam. Add the decorative balls.
2. Wire the decorating foam to the purchased wreath.

Feathers and Pinecone Gift Wraps

Unconventional nature-inspired wrapping papers and trims give new personality to holiday gifts.

WHAT YOU NEED
Old sheet music • Wrapping paper • Burlap ribbon • Pinecones • Feathers • Ribbon • Greenery pieces • Hot-glue gun and glue sticks

WHAT YOU DO
1. Wrap gifts as desired using wrapping paper or old sheet music. Cut ribbons to fit around packages. Layer and glue in place.
2. Add pinecones, feathers, ribbon, and bits of greenery as desired, and glue in place.

Holiday Paper

Celebrate the beauty of paper in your holiday crafting this year.
Whether you prefer delicate vellum and doilies or colorful
cardstock and printed papers on rolls—you'll find the perfect
paper craft to say "Merry Christmas!"

Vellum Greeting Cards

Pretty vellum paper can be stitched to purchased blank cards to create one-of-a-kind greetings for all the favorite people on your Christmas card list.

WHAT YOU NEED (for both cards)
Purchased blank card in desired colors • Decorative paper • Spray glue • Vellum and/or waxed paper • Embroidery thread • Embellishments such as star or flat beads

WHAT YOU DO

For the Tree Card:
1. Cut decorative paper to the size of your card and affix with spray glue.
2. Cut triangles of various sizes from vellum and/or waxed paper. Line them up on the card as desired. Hand-stitch through the bottom of the card, adding triangles as you go up.
3. Add a bead or star to the tree top. **Tip:** Use a mixture of vellum and waxed paper to give the tree an organic look.

For the Garland Card:
1. Cut decorative paper to the size of your card and affix with spray glue.
2. Cut squares, all the same size, out of vellum. Fold each in half forming a triangle. Hand-stitch a few lines across your card, attaching the triangles. **Tip:** To make hand stitching easier, first run the card and vellum pieces separately through an unthreaded sewing machine to create the holes.

Pierced Paper Luminarias

Let the light sparkle through tiny holes in beautiful papers that you wrap around glowing candles.

WHAT YOU NEED
Glass container • Gold decorative paper with tone-on-tone pattern • White vellum • Needle • Sewing machine (optional) • Narrow ribbon • Scalloped scissors • Crafts glue

WHAT YOU DO

For the Gold Luminaria:
Measure and cut decorative paper large enough to wrap around the glass container. Using a needle, poke holes about $\frac{1}{16}$ inch apart following pattern on paper. Embellish with ribbon.

For the White Luminaria:
1. Measure and cut four strips of vellum about 1½ inches tall and long enough to wrap around the diameter of the glass container. Using scalloped scissors, trim the tops of the paper strips. Run each strip through an unthreaded sewing machine twice, using the basic stitch. **Note:** This can be done by hand if you don't have a sewing machine.
2. Wrap each strip around the glass container, gluing strips together at the back. Embellish with ribbon.

Never leave a burning candle unattended.

Boxed Star Origami Ornament

 **1**

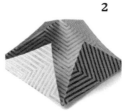 **2**

 **3**

 **4**

Boxed Star and Butterfly Origami Ornaments

Folded origami paper and beads magically combine to create stunning paper trims for your holiday tree.

For the Boxed Star:

WHAT YOU NEED

Lightweight decorative paper or origami paper • Fine string or twine • Beads: One large faceted jewel or bead and one small bead • Crafts glue

WHAT YOU DO

1. Cut six 3×3-inch squares out of decorative paper or origami paper.
2. Fold the paper in half, corner to corner, both ways to form crease lines through the center. See Photo 1, above.
2. Fold opposite corners (left and right) to meet in the center. See Photo 2, above.
3. Fold opposite corners (top and bottom) to meet each other. See Photo 3, above.
4. Using the crease lines to help, push in the two new corners formed to meet each other in the inside.
5. Repeat until you have six forms. Glue the flat edge of each form together until a circle is formed. See Photo 4, above.
6. Cut one section of string about 12 inches in length. String one faceted jewel or bead on string and slide it to the center of the string. String another bead, looping both ends of string into the bead. Run the string through the center of the ornament. Trim to desired length and tie on top of ornament to hang.

For the Butterfly Ornament:

WHAT YOU NEED

Lightweight decorative paper or origami paper • Fine string or twine • Beads: One large faceted jewel or bead and one small bead • Crafts glue

WHAT YOU DO

1. Cut six 3×3-inch squares out of decorative paper or origami paper.
2. Working with one piece of paper, fold the paper in half, both ways to form crease lines through the center. See Photo 1, below.
3. Fold opposite corners, left and right, to meet in the center. See Photo 2, below.
4. Fold opposite corners, top and bottom, to meet each other. See Photo 3, below.
5. Using the crease lines to help, push in the two new corners formed to meet each other in the inside. See Photo 4. Repeat until you have six forms. Glue the flat edges together until the butterfly shape is formed. See Photo 5, below.
6. Cut one section of string about 12 inches in length. String one bead on the string and slide it to the center of the string. String another bead, looping both ends of string into the bead. Run the string through the center of the ornament. Trim to desired length and tie on top of ornament to hang.

Butterfly Origami Ornament

 **1**

 **2**

 **3**

 **4**

 **5**

Dye-Dipped Doily Wreath

Doilies and dye combine ombre-style using Christmas green to create a soft, subtle, and beautiful wreath for holiday decorating.

WHAT YOU NEED

Food coloring • Water • Two small bowls • About 120 (4 packages) 4-inch white paper doilies • Hot-glue gun and glue sticks • Paper towels • 12-inch foam wreath form • 2 yards of 2-inch-wide white satin ribbon

WHAT YOU DO

1. Fill one small bowl with water only and the other bowl with 1 to 3 tablespoons of water and 3 to 6 drops of food coloring depending on desired color.

2. Hold a doily by the center and loosely fold it twice to form a triangle. Still holding the doily by the center, dip the lacy end first in the bowl of water and then in the food coloring solution. Continue this process with all doilies. **Note:** By dipping the doilies in water first, the color solution will slowly become more diluted as you continue dipping. Let doilies dry on paper towels.

3. When the doilies are dry, use hot glue to attach the center of the folded doilies to the foam wreath form, arranging colors from light to dark on the form. Tuck the doilies tightly as you glue them together. Let dry.

4. Tie a bow around the top of the wreath.

Whether you prefer to layer pastel doilies ombre-style for a ruffled wreath or create stand-up-straight paper trees in a little forest, using paper is just one way to make lovely decorations for your holiday home.

Pretty Paper Trees

Choose soft-tone papers and layer them like evergreen branches to create a delicate paper snow-covered forest to rest on a mantel or cupboard.

WHAT YOU NEED

Tracing paper • Pencil • Medium-weight scrapbook papers in desired colors • Scissors • Crafts glue • Snap-style clothespins • Wood skewers • Embellishments such as small adhesive-back jewels, pearl dots, and punched paper edging • Air-dry clay • Narrow ribbon in desired colors

WHAT YOU DO

1. Trace the patterns, below, and cut out. Cut out one small, one medium, and one large pattern for each tree from desired papers.
2. Curve the cut papers into cone shapes, leaving a tiny hole at the top. Use crafts glue to glue in place. Use a snap-style clothespin to hold in place until dry.
3. Embellish the cones as desired using paper punch strips, jewels, or other embellishments.
4. Make a walnut-size ball of clay. Cut a skewer to the desired length and place in the clay. Layer the cones by threading them onto the skewer. When in the desired position, place a small piece of clay at the cone top to secure.
5. Tie a bow with the ribbon and glue to the top of the tree.

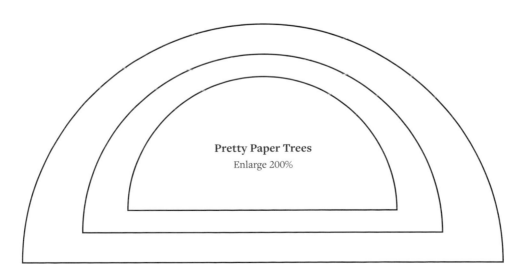

Pretty Paper Trees
Enlarge 200%

Choose your favorite wrapping and scrapbook papers, colorful thread, and easy stitches to create one-of-a-kind greeting cards for everyone on your holiday list.

Layered Ornament Card

Vellum circles are stitched onto a blank card and topped with a red bow to make a charming holiday greeting.

WHAT YOU NEED

Purchased blank card in desired color • Decorative paper • Spray glue • Vellum and/or waxed paper • Embroidery thread • Narrow red ribbon • Crafts glue

WHAT YOU DO

1. Cut decorative paper to the size of your card and affix with spray glue.
2. Cut six to ten same-size circles out of vellum and fold each in half. Stack all circles on top of one another and line them up on the card. Hand-stitch through the center of the circles up the top of the card. Tie ribbon into bow and glue to top of ornament.

Santa Greeting Cards

Whether you like to see Santa in person or just hear his "Ho-Ho-Ho" you'll love making these clever paper cards.

WHAT YOU NEED

Blank card • Decorative paper with Santa figure (for Santa Card only) • Spray glue • Wrapping paper • Embroidery thread • Letter stickers (for HO Card only) • Scalloped scissors • Crafts glue

WHAT YOU DO

For Santa Card:

1. Cut decorative paper using scalloped scissors to the size of your card and affix with spray glue.
2. Cut a circle out of wrapping paper with Santa figure and embellish using a simple back stitch and embroidery thread, following the pattern on your paper as a guide.
3. Cut a slightly larger circle out of another paper. Using a blanket stitch, embellish the outside of the circle. Adhere to card using crafts glue. **Note:** The divots in the scallop help stabilize your blanket stitch.

For the HO Card:

1. Cut decorative paper to the size of your card and affix with spray glue.
2. Affix letter stickers to card. Create a shadow by embroidering around the letter shape using the backstitch. Embroider the edge of the card using blanket stitch. (For Stitch Diagrams, see page 160.)

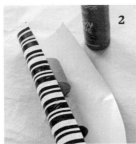

Wrapping Paper Poppers

Cardboard tubes are filled with candy, covered with wrapping paper, and tied with ribbons for sweet table favors.

WHAT YOU NEED

Paper towel rolls • Wrapping paper • Curling ribbon • Small wrapped candies • Scissors • Crafts glue

WHAT YOU DO

1. Cut a paper towel roll into three pieces. Each roll will make three poppers.

2. Cut each of the 3 pieces in half. Cut a piece of wrapping paper 8×11 inches. You will need one piece of paper for each popper.

3. Lay two of the tubes on the wrapping paper centering the tubes and leaving about 1 inch between the tubes. See Photo 1.

4. Roll the wrapping paper around the paper towel pieces and glue to secure. Fill the tube with candy. See Photo 2.

5. Squeeze one end of the paper together and tie with ribbon. Fill the open end with candy. See Photo 3.

6. Tie a ribbon around the other end. To "pop" the poppers, have guests break them in half to reveal the candy inside.

Tiered Tree

Red cardstock is punched and layered to make this lacy and delicate tree.

WHAT YOU NEED

Two pieces of 12-inch-square red cardstock • Paper trimmer • Scoring board • Scallop-edge border punch • Clear-drying glue • Hot-glue gun and glue sticks • Small ball ornament

WHAT YOU DO

1. Cut two 2½×12-inch strips from cardstock. Cut two 12-inch strips that are ⅛ inch narrower than the first strips, then cut two 12-inch strips ⅛ inch narrower than the second strips. Continue in the same manner, cutting two progressively narrower strips until all cardstock has been trimmed.

2. Lay a strip on the scoring board. Score crosswise lines spaced ½ inch apart along strip. Repeat with other strips. Punch one long edge of each strip with the scallop-edge punch. Accordion-fold the strips on scored lines. Use clear-drying glue to adhere the short edges of each strip pair together to make a circle (medallion). Squeeze the medallion together to close opening in center and secure with hot glue.

3. Repeat with the remaining strip pairs. To make the smaller medallions for the top third of tree, shorten the strips before joining pairs.

4. Hot-glue folded medallions together to make the tree shape, starting with the largest medallion at the bottom and ending with the smallest medallion at the top. To make a taller tree, fill in with some same-size medallions. Hot-glue a ball ornament to the top of the tree.

Straws and Cupcake Liner Garland

Striped paper straws, beads, and paper cupcake liners team up to make a charming holiday garland in no time!

WHAT YOU NEED

Striped paper straws • Paper cupcake liners in desired colors and patterns • Beads • Crafts glue • Waxed dental floss • Scissors

WHAT YOU DO

1. Cut the straws to desired lengths. Open and flatten cupcake liners. Fold liners in half.

2. Lay the straws, liners, and beads in the order that you want to string them. Starting with a bead, thread the floss through the bead and back through again and tighten with a knot.

3. Thread the straws and beads onto the floss, and glue the liners together around the floss. Make the garland as long as desired.

To-the-Point Package Topper

Elevate your package adornments from purchased mass-produced bows to works of art.

WHAT YOU NEED

Lightweight paper (such as photocopy or wrapping paper) in desired colors • Glass, mug, or circular lid to use as a template • Pencil • Crafts glue • Double-sided tape • Scissors

WHAT YOU DO

Make the Spikes:

1. Trace six circles onto lightweight paper, using a glass or circular lid as a template. **Note:** Circles that are 3 to 4 inches in diameter work best. For a two-color bow, cut three circles of each color. Cut out circles. Referring to photos, above, fold each circle in half, then in half again, and then in half a third time. Unfold and flatten circles. Each circle should have eight segments. Cut along each fold line three-fourths of the way to center of circle.

2. Roll each segment into a cone shape around a pencil tip with pencil tip pointing toward the outer edge of circle. Secure each cone shape with glue, pressing firmly until glue sets.

Assemble the Bow:

1. Place circles on a work surface with cone openings facing up, above. Place a dime-size amount of glue on center of each of five circles. With glue sides up, stack the circles on top of one another, placing so each layer's cones fit between cones of the previous layer. Place circle without glue (with cone openings up) on top of stack. Using the eraser end of a pencil, press down firmly in the center of the stack to form a curved shape; hold pencil in place until glue sets.

2. Apply double-sided tape to flat side of bow; press bow on gift by placing eraser end of the pencil through center of bow.

Custom Made

This year, make everyone's Christmas wishes
come true with handmade gifts designed and
created by you—especially for them.

Learning Pillow

He'll learn so much while he plays with his little felt pillow you made just for him!

WHAT YOU NEED

Two 16×16-inch squares of cream felt, such as National Nonwovens felt • 5×16-inch piece of blue felt • 4×12-inch piece of felt for boat • Two 5×10-inch pieces of felt in different colors for sails • Scraps of desired colored felt for sun, fish, and flower • Yellow-orange embroidery floss • Embroidery needle • Scrap of ribbon for flag and flower • 9-inch-long zipper • One large and one medium orange button • Small colored buttons for fish eyes • Scissors • Polyester fiberfill stuffing • Matching sewing thread

WHAT YOU DO

1. Lay the blue felt strip on the bottom of the cream felt pillow front and topstitch in place. Cut scallops around the edges of the front and back pieces.

2. Trace the boat pattern pieces, pages 74–75, onto desired colors of felt. Lay sail pieces side by side and topstitch zipper in the middle. Arrange the sails and other felt shapes on the pillow front. Machine-stitch around outside edges of the boat and sail using matching thread.

3. Cut flower, fish, and sun shapes from felt. Sew a 4-inch piece of ribbon to the flower back and to one side of the sail. Sew button over ribbon using embroidery floss. Make a slit in the flower for buttonhole.

4. Sew eyes on the fish shapes. Embroider sun rays for sun using backstitch. Sew large button for sun shape using embroidery floss. Make a slit for a buttonhole for the sun. Fold ribbon scrap in half for flag and tack to top of zipper.

5. Layer front and back, wrong sides facing. Topstitch through layers about 2 inches from each edge, leaving an opening at the bottom. Add stuffing. Stitch opening closed. **Note:** Zipper will open and fish can be stored inside of the sail pockets.

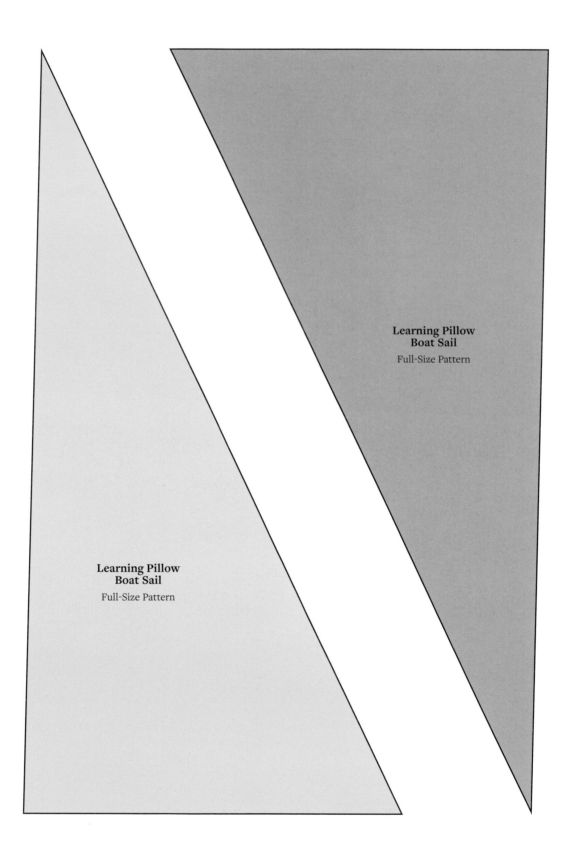

**Learning Pillow
Boat Sail**
Full-Size Pattern

**Learning Pillow
Boat Sail**
Full-Size Pattern

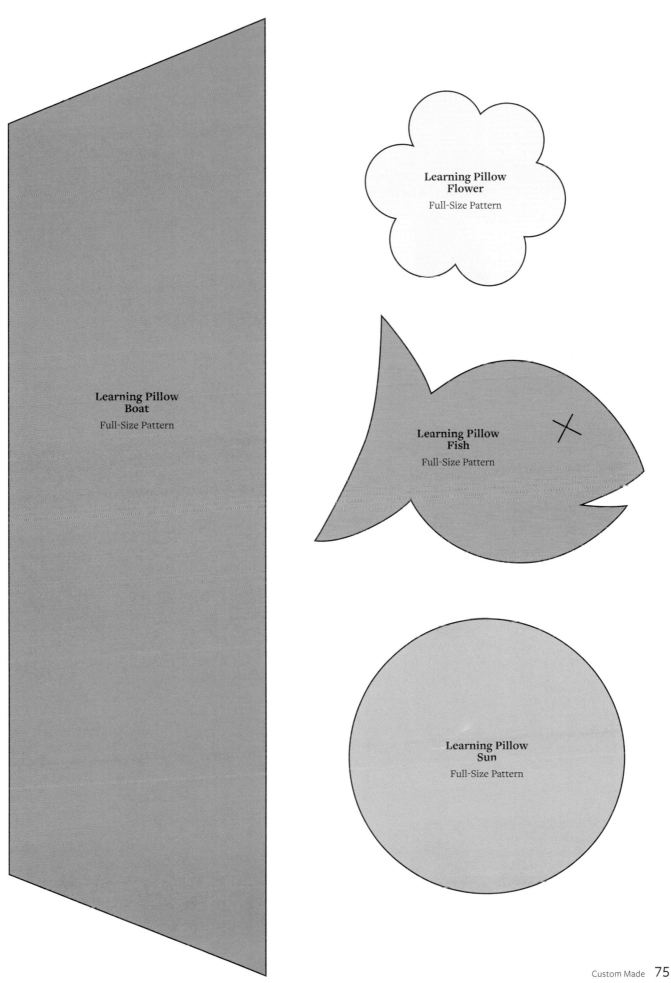

**Learning Pillow
Boat**

Full-Size Pattern

**Learning Pillow
Flower**

Full-Size Pattern

**Learning Pillow
Fish**

Full-Size Pattern

**Learning Pillow
Sun**

Full-Size Pattern

Oilcloth Tote

Oilcloth comes in vibrant colors and is perfect for holiday totes. Stitch one for that shop-til-you-drop friend this year!

WHAT YOU NEED

1 yard oilcloth fabric in desired print • 1 yard coordinating cotton fabric for lining • Cardboard for tote base • 1 yard white pom-pom trim • 2 yards white 1-inch webbing (for handles) • Scissors • Two large buttons • White sewing thread

WHAT YOU DO

1. Cut two 15-inch pieces of oilcloth for the tote body. Cut two 15-inch pieces of cotton fabric for the tote lining. Cut two strips of webbing each 32 inches long for the handles. Cut two $\frac{5}{8}$×32-inch strips of oilcloth for the decorative strap.

2. Fold the body piece of oilcloth in half with the right sides together. Stitch both side seams with a $\frac{1}{4}$-inch seam allowance. Using a long stitch length of about 8 stitches per inch is helpful when working with oilcloth. Clip seams open on both corners. Finger press the seams open at the corners.

3. Pinch the fabric at the bottom corner to make a triangle with the seam in the middle (the side and bottom seams will be matched up). Do this for both corners. Measure 1 inch from the point of each triangle and stitch through the layers of fabric, across the open seam, to form the box bottom and side corners of the tote. Clip off excess fabric triangles, trimming close to the stitching.

4. Clip the seams open on both sides and turn the piece right side out. Repeat steps 2 and 3 for the lining fabric. Leave the lining turned inside out. Finger-press the lining seams open.

5. Place the outside of the bag into the lining. Stitch around the top of the bag using a $\frac{3}{8}$-inch seam allowance. Leave the space between one of the handles open for turning. Trim the seam to $\frac{1}{4}$ inch. Turn the fabric right side out, pulling the fabric though the opening left at the top. Finger-press any seams.

6. To make a support piece for the base of the bag, cut a $3\frac{1}{2}$×11 inch rectangle from cardboard. Slip this through the opening to the bottom of the bag between the lining and outside layers.

7. Topstitch close to the edge around the top of the tote. This will close the opening as well as give the tote a finished look. Sew the decorative pom-pom trim close to the topstitched top edge. Turn the top edge down about 2 inches over the tote body.

8. To make the handles, topstitch the oilcloth strip to the webbing on both sides. Position the handles about 3 inches from the side seams on the inside of the bag. Stitch in place. Sew buttons to front of bag.

Doodle Initials

Have fun making little designs on purchased wood initials while you think about the special person.

WHAT YOU NEED

Purchased free-standing wood letter initials • Crafts paint in desired colors • Paintbrush • Fine-tip markers in desired colors

WHAT YOU DO

1. Be sure the letter is clean and dry. Lay the letter on a protected surface and paint with desired color. Let dry.

2. Use fine-tip markers to make small designs all over the painted letter. Let dry.

Crochet a cozy snowman hat for that special little person on your holiday list. It is sure to become a favorite friend for any boy or girl!

Happy Snowman Hat

What child wouldn't love to wear this adorable snowman hat? The piece is quick to make using chunky yarn and simple embellishments.

WHAT YOU NEED
One 6-ounce ball white chunky yarn, such as Red Heart Baby Clouds Yarn • Two accent color yarns, such as Red Heart acrylic yarn• Two black buttons • Scrap of black yarn • Orange felt • Scrap of orange yarn • Sewing needle large enough to accommodate yarn

WHAT YOU DO
Gauge: 3 stitches per inch

Body of Hat:
With white yarn:
Row 1: Ch 2. Crochet 9sc in 2nd ch from hook. Join with a sl st to first ch st.
Row 2: Ch 2, dc in same st, 2dc in next st and each around. Join with sl st to top of beginning.
Row 3: Ch 2, 2 dc in next st, dc in next, repeating pattern around hat. Join with sl st to top of beginning.
Row 4: Ch 2, 2 dc in next st, around. Join with sl st top of beginning.
Rows 5-10: Ch 2, dc in each st around hat. Continue to desired height, then join with sl st and fasten off.
Note: Depending on thickness of yarn used, you may want to chain more or less rows.

Accent Yarn:
Rows 11-14: Using accent color of yarn, sl st where white yarn ended to join. Ch 1, sc around hat. Continue to desired height, then join with sl st and fasten off.
Note: Depending on thickness of yarn used, you may want to chain more or less rows.

Headband:
In desired color of yarn, sc approx 40 st and fasten off.
Note: Depending on size of hat, you may want to make this longer or shorter. Make two pom-poms using the same color of yarn. Using same color of yarn, loosely sew the chain around the top of the hat and the pom-poms to the side.

Finishing:
Cut a triangle out of the orange felt and attach with a single stitch to the hat. Sew two black buttons on front for eyes using black yarn.

CROCHET ABBREVIATIONS

ch	chain
sl st	slip stitch
st(s)	stitch(es)
sc	single crochet
dc	double crochet

Child's Art Note Card Set

Let the little artists in your family create the artwork for a set of note cards that will be treasured forever!

WHAT YOU NEED

Children's artwork • Printed cardstock in desired color • Envelopes • White cardstock • Glue stick • Paper tape, such as Washi tape • Ribbon

WHAT YOU DO

1. Cut the printed cardstock to fold and fit into the desired purchased envelope. Make copies of the artwork onto cardstock, reducing or enlarging the artwork to fit the front of folded printed cardstock, leaving a ½-inch border around the edge. Adhere the drawing to the printed cardstock.
2. On the inside of the card, glue a smaller piece of white cardstock for writing. Run a strip of paper tape at the bottom for embellishment.
3. Stack up all of the cards and tie with a ribbon.

Message Frame

Keep it simple by using black and white to decorate a frame. It will complement any color scheme.

WHAT YOU NEED

Purchased white picture frame • Rubber stamp alphabet letters • Black stamp pad • Black dot adhesive stickers • Black and white paper tape, such as Washi tape • Scissors • Black and white photo or printed scrapbook message paper

WHAT YOU DO

1. Be sure the frame is clean and dry. Use the alphabet stickers and stamp pad to print desired words on the frame. Let dry.
2. Wrap the paper tape around the frame and embellish with black dot adhesive stickers.
3. Frame a photo or piece of paper in the frame.

Stamped Greeting Card Set

Use simple objects to stamp your holiday greetings this year. Everyone will love the message and your creativity!

WHAT YOU NEED

Box of solid color blank greeting cards • Scrap of lightweight-foam (for tree shape) • Wine bottle cork (for circle shapes) • Stencil paper (for Santa shapes) • Stencil brush • Acrylic paint in white, metallic gold, green, and red • Small paper doily • Fine-tip permanent pen or marker • Small adhesive pearls

WHAT YOU DO

For the Tree Card:
Cut a small tree shape from the foam. Stamp triangle tree shape using green acrylic paint. Use white paint and a stencil brush to paint through the doily. Remove doily. Add details with fine-tip black pen or marker. Add an adhesive pearl tree topper.

For the Snowman, Ornament, and Wreath Cards:
Stamp circles onto the cards using a wine bottle cork. Use metallic gold paint for the ornaments, white for the snowman, and green for the wreath. Draw details and words with fine-tip pen or marker. Add sticker pearls to the ornaments.

For the Santa Card:
Copy stencil patterns, left, onto stencil paper and cut out. Use the stencil brush and red and white paint to paint the pattern onto the blank card or tag. Remove stencil. Add details with fine-tip black pen or marker.

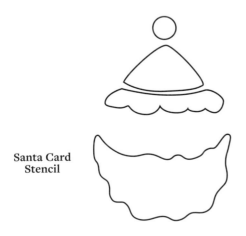

Santa Card
Stencil

Use stencilling and stamping techniques to make greeting cards by the dozen! Just use small objects you have on hand to create the stamps and add fine details using permanent marker.

Colorful Wraps

Combine bright wrapping papers, twine, buttons, and stickers to create wraps that are sure to make your season bright!

WHAT YOU NEED

Brightly colored wrapping paper • Baker's twine • Silk cording • Stickers • Jewels • Buttons • Ribbon • Paper tape, such as Washi tape • Transparent tape

WHAT YOU DO

1. Wrap the package in the desired paper. Embellish with wrapped twine, ribbon, or cording. Add paper tape or threaded buttons, securing with tape.

2. Add stickers to flat areas or adhere to the strings or ribbon. Add tag if desired.

Winter Sparkle

Bring the magic of Christmas into your home with handmade
crafts and decorations that shimmer and shine with the season.

GLITTERING STAR

METALLIC SNOWFLAKE

BEADED STAR

Christmas Eve Sparkle

Create some Christmas magic with a tree full of colorful sparkling trims. Wind a teal satin ribbon around the tree and surround it with glittered stars, metallic medallions, and wired stars and moons. Then wrap your packages in shimmering wraps and ribbons to tuck under the tree.

Glittering Star

Just a little dusting of tiny beads and glitter transforms papier mâché stars into sparkling trims.

WHAT YOU NEED

Star-shape papier mâché forms (available at crafts stores) • Spray paint • Glitter and/or mini beads to match paint • Decoupage medium such as Mod Podge • Paintbrush • Fine gold thread • Crafts glue

WHAT YOU DO

1. Spray paint the papier mâché star in desired color. When dry, apply a coat of decoupage medium to one side of star. Dust with glitter or mini beads. **Tip:** Use a thin to normal coat of decoupage medium for glitter; use a very thick coat for beads.
2. Glue a loop of fine gold thread for hanging.

Metallic Snowflake

Purchased snowflake ornaments are layered with medallions for a simple and stunning effect.

WHAT YOU NEED

Purchased metallic glitter snowflakes • Metal medallions • Small jewel (optional) • Hot-glue gun and glue sticks • Metallic gold ribbon

WHAT YOU DO

1. Plan the design and layer the pieces.
2. Using hot glue, adhere the pieces. Add a jewel to the center if desired. Glue a ribbon at the top for a hanger.

Beaded Star

Beads line up on wires to surround a glittered ball to form sparkling beaded trims.

WHAT YOU NEED

26 gauge wire • Wire cutters • Beads in various sizes • Wooden split balls • Hot glue gun • Glitter • Crafts glue

WHAT YOU DO

1. Begin by making the star frame. Cut four sections of wire, all 6 to 8 inches in length. Hot-glue the center of each wire section onto one wooden split ball. See Photo A.
2. When hot glue is dry, glue another wooden split ball on top, forming a sphere. Brush crafts glue on wooden ball and dust with glitter.
3. When glitter is dry, stack beads onto the wires until desired length is reached. See Photo B. Trim the wire flush with the end of the final bead. Dab a spot of hot glue at the end to secure the bead strand on the wire. Repeat for all wires. Be sure to leave one wire long for the hanger. On this strand, do not trim. Dot with hot glue and bend the excess wire to form the hanger.

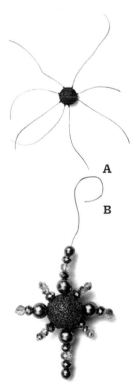

A

B

BEADED MOON
ORNAMENT

BEADED STAR
TREE TOPPER

Bead and wire combine to make celestial trims for your holiday tree. Choose bead colors and styles to make your tree one in a million.

Beaded Moon Ornament

A bit of wire and a few beads make an ethereal moon-shape ornament to add shimmer and shine to your tree.

WHAT YOU NEED
26 gauge wire • Wire cutters • Beads in various sizes

WHAT YOU DO
1. Cut a piece of wire about 20 inches long depending on the size of your ornament.
2. Leaving about 4 inches of wire at the top, wrap the wire around a round object twisting and joining the ends together at the top. **Tip:** A spray paint can works well. See Illustration 1.
3. Tighten the twist and remove wire from form carefully. See Illustration 2.
4. Bend the wire down toward the bottom of the circle. String beads until the bottom of the circle is reached. See Illustration 3.
5. String your final bead. Bend the wire straight up and wrap it around itself to stabilize. See Illustration 4.
6. Trim end of wire. Bend the top wire to form a hook. See Illustration 5.

Beaded Star Tree Topper

Made in a similar fashion to the Star Ornaments, this stunning piece uses a large foam ball for the center and skewers of glittered beads.

WHAT YOU NEED
24 gauge wire • Wire cutters • Beads in various sizes • 2-inch foam ball, such as Styrofoam • Hot-glue gun and glue sticks • Wooden skewers • Glitter • Crafts glue

WHAT YOU DO
1. Make the star frame. Cut four sections of wire, all 8 to 10 inches in length.
2. Cut the foam ball in half. Hot-glue the center of each wire section onto one half of the ball.
3. Cut wooden skewers into eight 3- to 4-inch long sections. Glue each skewer onto the foam ball between each wire section.
4. When hot glue is dry, glue the other half of foam ball on top, forming a sphere. Brush crafts glue on foam ball and wooden skewers; dust with glitter.
5. When glitter is dry, start stacking beads onto the wire until desired length is reached. Trim the wire flush with the end of the final bead. Dab a spot of hot glue at the end to secure the bead stand on the wire. Repeat for all wires. Be sure to leave one wire long; this will be the wire you attach the tree topper to the tree. On this strand, don't trim, just dot with hot glue. Attach a bead at the end of each skewer.

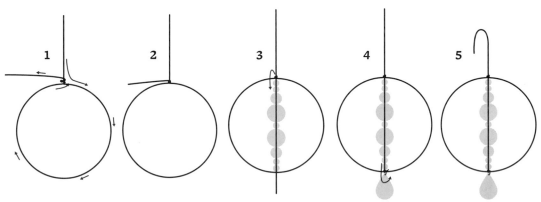

1   2   3   4   5

Sparkling Champagne Tree

Clear glass balls, some with tiny jingle bells inside, adorn a tree with golden light. Combining copper and clear glass balls with white twinkling light makes a glistening display in any room. Add a clear glass vintage bowl filled with clear ornaments in different sizes and shapes to add more magical Christmas sparkle.

Easy Jingle Bells Trim

A few golden jingle bells and a clear glass ball is all it takes to make this simple sparkling trim.

WHAT YOU NEED
Clear glass ball with removable top • Gold jingle bells small enough to fit into the ball • ¼-inch-wide gold ribbon

WHAT YOU DO
1. Be sure the glass ball is clean and dry. Gently remove the ornament hanger top. Carefully fill with jingle bells. Put hanger top back on ornament.
2. Thread the ribbon through the hanger and tie with a bow for hanging.

Message Candles

Alphabet stickers spell out messages of peace and joy on a lovely votive candle display.

WHAT YOU NEED
Clear glass votive candle holders • Towel • Alphabet stickers • Star stickers • Tea light candles • Clear glass tray

WHAT YOU DO
1. Be sure the votive holders are clean and dry. For support, lay the candle holder on a towel and carefully adhere the alphabet stickers to the front, spelling the desired word. Add a star sticker on each side of each word.
2. Place the votive holders on the clear glass tray. Place a tea candle in each one. Light the candles.

Never leave a burning candle unattended.

Spheres of Light Candle

Like bubbles of glass, a silver candle is surrounded by spheres of light.

WHAT YOU NEED
2 clear glass plates • Silver pillar candle • Clear glass ornament balls in various sizes

WHAT YOU DO
1. Be sure the plates and ornaments are clean and dry. Stack the two plates atop each other.
2. Place the candle on the plates and surround with the glass balls.

Never leave a burning candle unattended.

Shimmering Magnolia Wreath

Magnolia leaves are painted and layered on a wreath form to create a stunning holiday wreath.

WHAT YOU NEED

Magnolia leaves • Paintbrush • Paint in desired colors including metallic gold • Hot-glue gun and glue sticks • Glitter • 14-inch foam wreath form such as Styrofoam • 2½-inch-wide gold ribbon

WHAT YOU DO

1. Cut magnolia leaves off of stem/branch. Using a paintbrush, paint the backs of the leaves with paint or with glue then dust with glitter. Let dry.
2. Layer the leaves on the wreath form using hot glue in an alternating pattern spacing out the colors used. Tie a bow with the ribbon and hot glue at the top.

Glittered Package Tops

A little glue and some fine glitter is all it takes to make your Christmas boxes sparkle for the season.

WHAT YOU NEED

• White paper (optional) • Purchased or wrapped boxes • Crafts glue • Fine glitter in desired colors • Scrap of ribbon or purchased bow (optional) • Purchased tag (optional)

WHAT YOU DO

1. Plan the design on the box top by practicing first on a piece of white paper, if desired.
2. Draw the design on the box using glue. Dust with glitter. Shake off any excess glitter. Add bows, if desired. Embellish the tag and add, if desired.

Scandinavian Influence

Holiday cheer shifts to refreshing Nordic style with projects made from wool felt, paper, and simple stitches. The look is understated and modern, yet cozy and comforting.

DRAWN NORDIC
DESIGN WRAP

EMBELLISHED RIBBON
AND CARDBOARD FLOWER

DOILY WRAP

FELT CIRCLES WRAP

FELT TRIANGLE WRAP

Scandinavian Gift Wrap

Traditional Nordic red, white, ice blue, and natural tan colors inspire this stack of too-pretty-to-open gifts.

WHAT YOU NEED

Nonwoven felt, such as National Nonwovens in red • Pom-poms • Purchased cotton doily • Embroidery thread • Embroidery needle • Plain ribbon • Decorative ribbon • Cardboard tube • Scissors • Hot-glue gun and glue sticks • Fine-tip permanent marker • Brown kraft paper

WHAT YOU DO

For the Felt Triangle Wrap:
Attach felt triangles onto wrapped gift using hot glue. Add decorative ribbon and a pom-pom to the top.

For the Doily Wrap:
String ribbon through a doily and tie at the back of the package.

For the Embellished Ribbon and Cardboard Flower:
Embellish plain ribbon using embroidery thread and simple stitches such as cross stitch and running stitch. For Stitch Diagrams, see page 160. To make the flower, fold a cardboard tube lengthwise and cut it into five equal pieces. Glue the ends together with hot glue and attach to gift.

For the Drawn Nordic Design Wrap:
Use a fine-tip black marker to embellish brown kraft paper wrapping. Using the pattern, above right, as a guide, fill paper with design. Embellish plain ribbon using embroidery thread and simple stitches such as the straight stitch. Tie around wrapped package.

For the Felt Circles Wrap:
Cut circles out of red felt. Using white embroidery thread and referring to the designs, right, stitch patterns onto felt rounds. Hot-glue to ribbon and wrap around box.

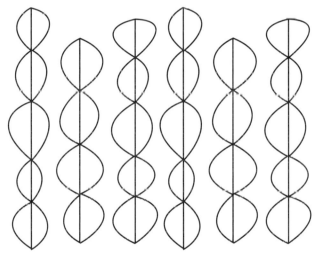

Drawn Nordic Design Wrap Designs

Felt Circles Wrap Patterns

Tiny boxes take on Nordic charm when decoupaged with copies of vintage postcards and colorful Scandinavian stamps. Use the backs and fronts of the postcards to showcase heartfelt messages.

Scandinavian Decoupage Boxes

Vintage postcards and letters are lovingly decoupaged onto little boxes to create heirloom-quality pieces.

WHAT YOU NEED

Unfinished balsa wood boxes (available in different sizes/shapes at crafts stores) • Acrylic paint in desired colors • Postage stamps • Vintage postcards • Decoupage medium, such as Mod Podge • Paintbrush • Screwdriver • Scissors

WHAT YOU DO

1. Remove hinges and clasps from the boxes. Paint boxes using acrylic paint.
2. Make color copies of the stamps and the postcards. Using the decoupage medium, add stamps in a lined-up fashion, trailing over the sides and front of box.
3. Use decoupage to adhere postcards onto boxes, pressing the paper into grooves. If decoupaging a curved lid, coat paper with decoupage to increase its flexibility, and then let the paper naturally fold over. Reapply decoupage and smooth with fingers or brush. Let dry. Put hinges and clasps back on boxes.

Snowflake Stocking

Easy-to-use wool felt is a Christmas crafter's best friend. Red felt stockings are dressed up with snowflakes on the toes and heels, and roses on the cuffs. The flowers are strips of ivory felt rolled into spirals.

WHAT YOU NEED

Two 10×14-inch pieces red wool felt • Beige and ivory wool felt scraps • Felt glue, such as Beacon Felt Glue • Red sewing thread • Three rolled felt roses

WHAT YOU DO

1. Enlarge the stocking front/back, cuff, snowflake, toe piece, and partial snowflake patterns, right; cut out. Using the patterns, cut two front/back pieces and a snowflake from red felt and the toe piece and partial snowflake from beige felt.

2. Adhere the toe piece to the stocking front using felt glue; let dry. Adhere the snowflake to the toe piece and the partial snowflake to the heel with felt glue; let dry.

3. With right sides facing, pin the two stocking front/back pieces together. Using ¼-inch seam allowances, sew stocking front/back piece together, leaving the top open and about 1 inch below the top on both sides. Turn stocking inside out and press.

4. Using the pattern, cut two cuffs from red felt. Turn inside out and sew sides together, using ¼-inch seam allowances; press. With wrong sides facing, pin the cuff to the stocking, gathering the cuff slightly to fit. Sew the cuff and stocking together using ¼-inch seam allowance. Turn right side out, and fold the cuff about 4 inches over stocking top.

5. Use felt glue to attach three rolled felt roses (see instructions in Flower Wreath, page 111) to the cuff. For a hanger, cut a ¾×7-inch strip of red felt; sew to the inside left of the cuff. Press stocking.

Delicate white roses made from ivory felt top a Christmas-red felt stocking. The red-and-ivory stocking is adorned with snowflakes on the toe and heel for a wintery Nordic look.

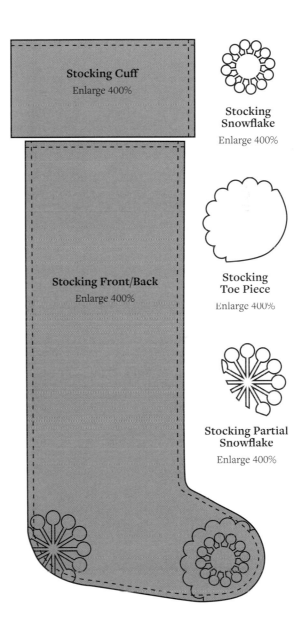

Stocking Cuff
Enlarge 400%

Stocking Front/Back
Enlarge 400%

Stocking Snowflake
Enlarge 400%

Stocking Toe Piece
Enlarge 400%

Stocking Partial Snowflake
Enlarge 400%

TREE TOPPER

CLAY REINDEER
ORNAMENT

FELT HONEYCOMB
ORNAMENTS

Restrained Beauty

A simple tree with casual ornamentation reveals the beauty of Scandinavian design. For this look, purchase a Nordic-style tree and place it in a galvanized tub. The decorations—a star topper and honeycomb ornaments all crafted from wool felt—add warmth. Clay reindeer cut with a cookie cutter add additional homemade touches.

Tree Topper

WHAT YOU NEED

Red wool felt, such as National Nonwovens • Embroidery and sewing needles • Pins • Red sewing thread • Fiberfill • Red embroidery floss • ¾-inch-diameter wooden ball with center hole

WHAT YOU DO

1. Enlarge the star pattern, page 108, and cut out. Using the pattern, cut two stars from red felt. Fold along dashed line and press.
2. Stitch ⅛-inch tucks along the pressed folds, alternating the tucks to the right side and wrong side. With wrong sides facing, pin the star shapes together. Sew the shapes together approximately ⅛ inch from the edges, leaving a 3-inch opening.
3. Stuff the star with fiberfill; sew the opening closed. Using embroidery floss, attach the wooden ball to the center of the star. Pull the thread tightly and knot on the back side. Leave the tails long to tie the star to the treetop.

Clay Reindeer Ornament

WHAT YOU NEED

Air-dry clay, such as Crayola Air-Dry Clay • Rolling pin • Reindeer cookie cutter • Doily • Burnisher • Drinking straw • ¼-inch-wide red ribbon

WHAT YOU DO

1. Roll a lump of air-dry clay into a ball. Using the rolling pin, flatten the clay to ³⁄₁₆-inch thickness. Using the cookie cutter, cut out reindeer shape. Press a doily into the clay. Roll over the doily with a burnisher to get an even imprint.
2. Using the straw, punch a hanging hole at a spot where the ornament will hang evenly. Let the clay dry thoroughly. Thread the ribbon through the hole and tie to form a hanging loop.

Felt Honeycomb Ornaments

WHAT YOU NEED

Wool felt, such as National Nonwovens in red, ivory, taupe, or beige • ½-inch-wide rayon ribbon in red, ivory, or light brown • Sewing needle • Ivory and red sewing thread • 2¾-inch-diameter wooden beads

WHAT YOU DO

1. Enlarge desired honeycomb ornament pattern, page 108, and cut out pattern piece. Using the pattern, cut eight pieces of the same shape from the same color of felt. Stack all eight shapes on top of each other.
2. Cut ribbon the length of the ornament plus about 3 to 4 inches for a tail and 8 inches for a loop. Form a 4-inch loop at the top of the ribbon; position the ribbon along the center of the ornament, leaving a short tail.
3. Using ivory thread, sew down the center of the stack, joining all eight layers and the ribbon. Press open each layer. Referring to the stitching diagram, below, hand-stitch every other layer in honeycomb fashion at 1-inch intervals along the edges.
4. Slide one bead down the ribbon loop to the top of the ornament. Slide the other bead up the ribbon tail to the ornament bottom, knotting the ribbon directly under the bead.

Stitching Diagram

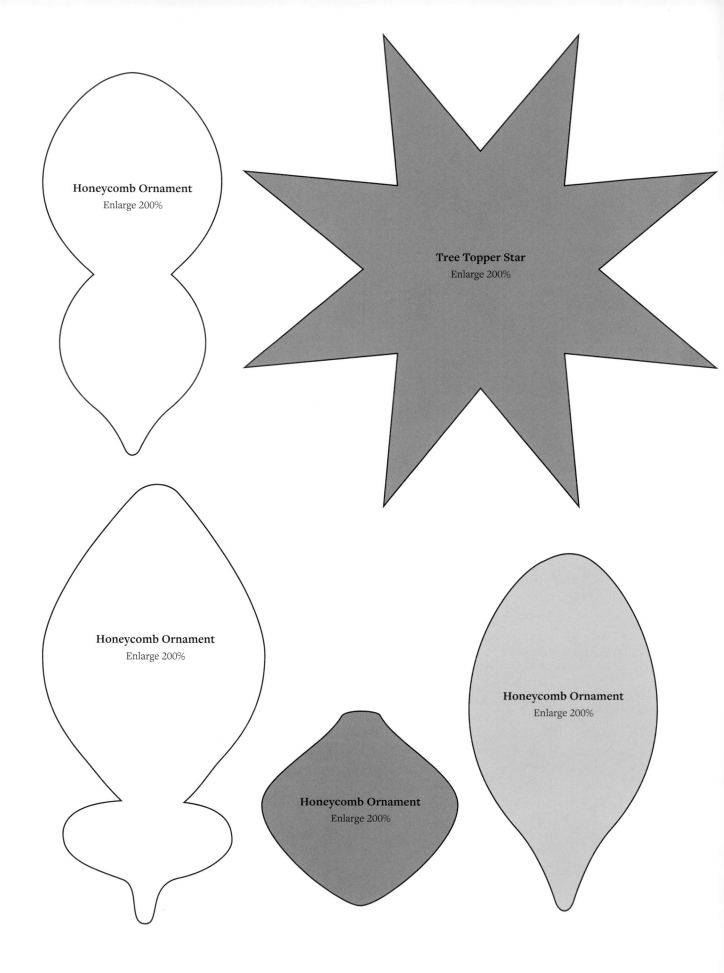

Honeycomb Ornament
Enlarge 200%

Tree Topper Star
Enlarge 200%

Honeycomb Ornament
Enlarge 200%

Honeycomb Ornament
Enlarge 200%

Honeycomb Ornament
Enlarge 200%

So Deer Pillow

Toss a seasonal pillow on a chair or bed to get any room in the holiday spirit. Deer—a recurring Scandinavian motif—brighten the accent pillow.

WHAT YOU NEED
Wool felt, such as National Nonwovens in red and ivory • Ivory embroidery floss • Embroidery and sewing needles • Felt glue • Fiberfill • Red sewing thread • 14 ivory felted wool balls

WHAT YOU DO
1. Cut two 15×8-inch rectangles from red felt. Using ivory embroidery floss, blanket-stitch the rectangles together, leaving an opening for fiberfill.
2. Enlarge the reindeer pattern, right. Cut out. Cut two reindeer from ivory felt, reversing the pattern for one of the pieces. Using felt glue, adhere the reindeer facing each other to the pillow front; let dry.
3. Lightly stuff pillow with fiberfill; blanket-stitch opening closed. Using red sewing thread, attach seven felt balls evenly spaced at each end of the pillow.

So Deer Pillow
Enlarge 200%

Frame of Reference

An ivory wreath crafted from felt flowers stands out in a red frame. Deer-motif felt pouches make perfect party favors. Fill the pouches with tea bags or add any little treat you like.

Flower Wreath

WHAT YOU NEED
Ivory wool felt, such as National Nonwovens • Felt glue • Ivory embroidery floss • Small wood beads • Sewing needle • Ivory sewing thread • Corrugated cardboard • Six ivory felted wool balls

WHAT YOU DO
Trace poinsettia and rose patterns, right, and cut out. Cut flowers from wool felt. Repeat the instructions, which are for a single flower, the number of times desired for your wreath. This wreath has one each small, medium, and large poinsettia; four large roses; four small roses; and two carnations.

For a Medium Poinsettia:
Cut seven medium petals. Arrange petals in a flower shape; glue together using felt glue. Let dry. Using embroidery floss, thread together six or seven beads. Using the needle and thread, stitch the cluster to the center of the flower.

For a Large Poinsettia:
Cut seven medium petals from ivory felt. Assemble the same as for the medium poinsettia. Cut seven large petals from ivory felt. Arrange the large petals in a flower shape; adhere together using felt glue. Glue the medium-petal flower atop the large-petal flower so the medium petals fall in between the large ones. Let dry.

For a Small Poinsettia:
Cut five medium petals and assemble the same as the medium-size poinsettia.

For a Small Rose:
Cut a spiral from the felt, as shown on pattern. Roll the spiral on its edge into a flower and glue along the bottom edge to hold its shape. Glue the bottom of the flower to a 2-inch-diameter felt circle. Let dry.

For a Large Rose:
Cut a spiral from the felt as shown on the pattern and roll. Glue the bottom of the flower to a 3-inch-diameter felt circle. Cut six petals and glue them around the outer edges of the rolled flower. Let dry.

For a Carnation:
Cut a 1×8-inch strip from ivory felt. Snip into the strip to make a fringe, leaving about ¼ inch uncut. Roll the strip into a flower shape, forming a tight center and loose outer "petals." Use felt glue to hold the shape. Let dry.

Cut cardboard into a 12-inch-diameter wreath form that is 2 inches wide. Arrange the flowers on the wreath form. Using felt glue, attach the flowers to the wreath. Fill in bare spots by gluing on felted wool balls.

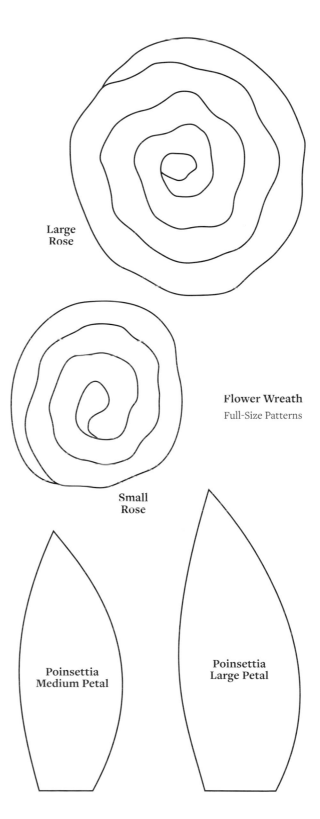

Large Rose

Flower Wreath
Full-Size Patterns

Small Rose

Poinsettia Medium Petal

Poinsettia Large Petal

Tea Bag Pouch

WHAT YOU NEED

Red and beige wool felt, such as National Nonwovens •
Embroidery and sewing needles • Beige sewing thread
• Red embroidery floss • ¾-inch-diameter wooden
button • Felt glue, such as Beacon Felt Glue

WHAT YOU DO

1. Enlarge tea bag pouch patterns, below; cut out pattern
pieces. Using patterns, cut one body from beige felt and
the flap and reindeer head from red felt.

2. With right sides together, sew flap to body along the
sewing line, leaving a ³⁄₁₆-inch seam allowance. Fold flap
over; press. Fold pouch on fold line; press. Cut slit on flap
where indicated for the button hole. Using embroidery
floss, sew the button in place and use the blanket stitch to
connect sides of pouch together. (For Stitch Diagrams, see
page 160.) Glue reindeer head to back of pouch; let dry.

Tea Bag Pouch
Enlarge 133%

Reindeer Head

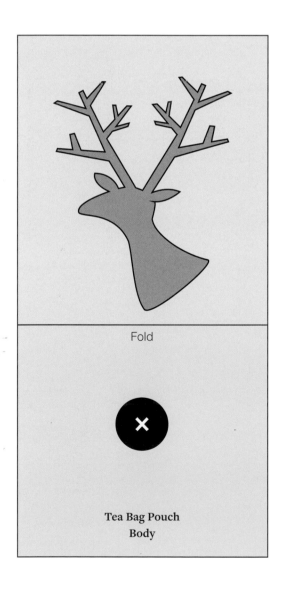

Fold

**Tea Bag Pouch
Body**

**Tea Bag Pouch
Flap**

Cut slit

Pom-Pom Trim Charger

WHAT YOU NEED

Red wool felt, such as National Nonwovens • Ivory embroidery floss • Embroidery and sewing needles • Red sewing thread • 36 red felted wool balls

WHAT YOU DO

Cut two 12-inch-diameter circles from red felt. Using embroidery floss, blanket-stitch the circles together. Using sewing thread, hand-stitch the felted wool balls, about 1¼ inches apart, to the edges of the joined circles.

Flower Chairback with Pillow

This merry red accent makes dining chairs comfy to sit on and pretty to look at from behind. A felt strap draped over each chair back holds a pillow on one end and a flower decoration on the other.

WHAT YOU NEED

Wool felt, such as National Nonwovens in beige, red, and ivory • Red embroidery floss • Felt glue, such as Beacon Felt Glue • Embroidery and sewing needles • Ivory sewing thread • 1-inch-diameter beige felted wool ball • Reindeer accent pillow, page 109

WHAT YOU DO

1. Enlarge the petals, petal background, and flower back patterns; cut out pattern pieces. Cut the flower back from red felt, the petal background from beige, and six petals from ivory. Using red embroidery floss, blanket-stitch around the petal background. Glue the petal background to the flower back. Using thread, make a small stitch at the end of each petal to give it shape. Glue the petals to the petal background, attaching them at the stitched ends. Glue the felted wool ball in the center.

2. Cut a 2½-inch-wide strap from ivory felt, making it long enough to drape over the chairback and attach to the pillow. Place a strap end inside a small opening in the pillow top. Blanket-stitch the strap and pillow together, catching the strap inside the pillow. Glue the assembled flower to the other end of the strap.

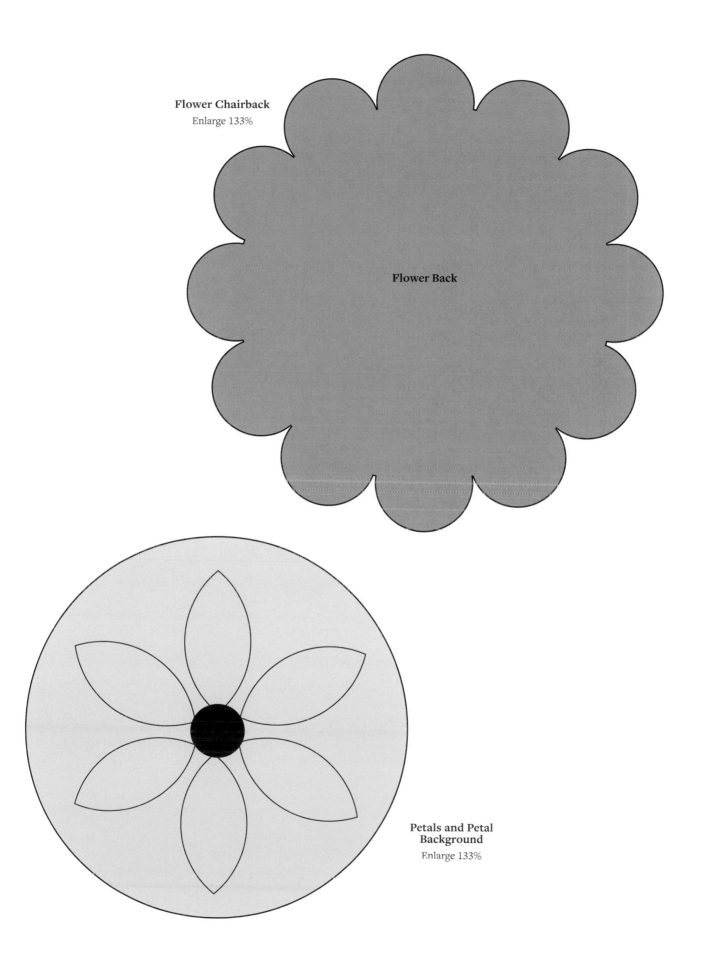

Flower Chairback
Enlarge 133%

Flower Back

Petals and Petal Background
Enlarge 133%

Advent Calendar Tree and Ornaments

WHAT YOU NEED

For the Tree:
Wool felt, such as National Nonwovens in red, beige, taupe, and ivory • Felt glue, such as Beacon Felt Glue • 1-inch thick insulated sheathing (26×36 inches) • 24 one-inch shaker pegs • Saw • Hot-glue gun and glue sticks • 2-inch wooden numbers (1 through 24) • Sewing needle • Ivory sewing thread • Two ivory felted wool balls

WHAT YOU DO

1. Cut red felt to measure 30×40 inches. Glue red felt to sheathing, gluing excess felt to the back side. Enlarge the Advent calendar tree (including the peg locations), trunk, and star patterns, page 118. Cut out. Using the patterns, cut the tree from beige felt, the trunk from taupe felt, and the star from ivory felt.

2. Using glue, attach tree and trunk shapes to red felt; let dry. Cut shanks off pegs with a saw. Mark peg locations with a pen on the tree and hot-glue pegs in place. Using felt glue, attach the star at the top of the tree.

3. Hot-glue 2-inch wooden numbers 1 through 24 in their respective spots (they will become visible each day as an ornament is removed). With a needle and thread, hang felted wool balls on the tree branches.

WHAT YOU NEED

For the Ornaments:
Ivory wool felt, such as National Nonwovens • Embroidery needle • Red embroidery floss • Fiberfill • 24 small curtain hook tie-back pins • Aluminum foil tape • Two 1-inch-diameter wooden balls • 1½-inch wooden numbers (1 through 24)

WHAT YOU DO

1. Enlarge ornament and ornament back pocket patterns, below, and cut out. Using patterns, cut 48 ornament circles and 24 ornament back pockets from ivory felt. Stack two ornament circles and a back pocket. Using embroidery floss, blanket-stitch the three pieces together on the edges, leaving an opening at the top. Fill each ornament lightly with fiberfill and blanket-stitch the opening closed.

2. Hook a curtain hook tie-back pin to the stitching at each ornament top. Wrap the base of the pin with aluminum foil tape. Repeat for remaining ornaments. Using felt glue, attach a wooden number to each of 24 assembled ornaments. Put a piece of candy or small treat in the back pocket. Hang each ornament on its corresponding peg.

Advent Calendar Ornament Back Pocket

Enlarge 200%

Advent Calendar Ornament

Enlarge 200%

Advent Calendar
Tree, Trunk, and Star
Enlarge 200%

Wooden Biscuit Tree

Layers of wooden biscuits create a simple yet stunning Nordic tree for your holiday decor.

WHAT YOU NEED

6-inch-tall foam cone, such as Styrofoam Cone • Size 10 wooden biscuits (found at home improvement stores) • Hot-glue gun and glue sticks • Natural buttons

WHAT YOU DO

1. Starting at the bottom of the cone, glue biscuits around the bottom of the tree in a straight line, letting the bottom edge of the biscuit hang over the bottom edge of the cone.
2. Continue, row by row, working your way up the tree.
Tip: The biscuits may not line up perfectly around the tree. Identify a "back" to the tree before you begin. Each time you start gluing a row of biscuits on, start at the back and work your way around.
3. Adhere a button to the top for a tree topper.

Festive Gifts from the Kitchen

An edible gift made by hand—be it sweet or savory—is a gift from the heart. Not only are you giving something delicious to eat, but you are also giving the time you spent making it.

Mint-Chocolate Trees

No special cutters or tools are needed to make these charming tree-shape treats. Two differently flavored and colored doughs are layered and formed into a log, then shaped and sliced.

WHAT YOU NEED
- ¾ cup butter, softened
- 1 cup sugar
- ½ teaspoon baking powder
- ¼ teaspoon salt
- 1 egg
- 1 teaspoon mint extract
- 2 cups all-purpose flour
- 2 ounces semisweet chocolate, melted
  Green paste food coloring
- 1 cup pecan halves

WHAT YOU DO

1. In a large mixing bowl beat butter with an electric mixer on medium to high speed for 30 seconds. Add sugar, baking powder, and salt. Beat until combined, scraping sides of bowl occasionally. Beat in egg and mint extract until combined. Beat in as much of the flour as you can with the mixer. Stir in any remaining flour. Divide dough in half. Stir melted chocolate into half of the dough. Knead the green food coloring into the remaining half of the dough. If necessary, cover and chill dough about 1 hour or until easy to handle.

2. Divide the green dough in half. Shape each dough half into a 10-inch log. Flatten the sides of the logs so they have three flat sides and are triangular. Wrap each triangular log in plastic wrap. Chill about 1 hour or until dough is firm.

3. Divide the chocolate dough in half. Between two sheets of waxed paper, roll half of dough into a 10×4-inch rectangle. Remove top sheet of waxed paper. Place one chilled green log in the center of the chocolate rectangle. Using the waxed paper, bring the sides of the chocolate rectangle up over the green log to enclose; press sides to seal. Repeat with the remaining chocolate dough and green log. Wrap logs in plastic wrap; freeze at least 1 hour or overnight.

4. Preheat oven to 375°F. Line a cookie sheet with parchment paper. Using a sharp knife, cut logs into ¼-inch-thick slices. If necessary, rotate log every few slices to keep its triangular shape. Place slices 2 inches apart on the prepared cookie sheet. Press a pecan half into the bottom edge of each triangle slice as a tree trunk. Bake for 6 to 8 minutes or until tops are set. Transfer to a wire rack and let cool. Place cookies in gift bags. Makes about 72 cookies.

To Make Ahead: Layer cookies between sheets of waxed paper in an airtight container; cover. Store at room temperature for up to 3 days or freeze for up to 3 months.

HOW TO MAKE THIS FOOD GIFT
Add cookies to a decorative paper bag (A) and wrap a corrugated easy-wrap ribbon (B) around the bag. Apply washi tape (C) to the center of the ribbon. Cut a circle from kraft paper (D), write a message, and attach to the center of the bag with a glue stick. Tie a hemp string (E) around the bag as a finishing touch.

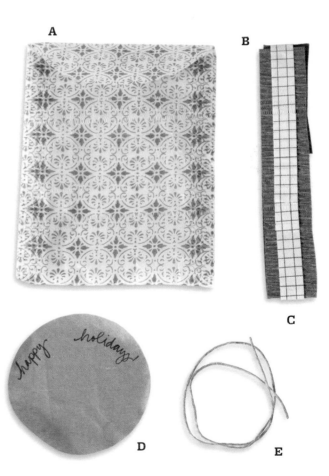

Salted Chocolate-Caramel Clusters

These tasty turtle-shape candies have a finishing sprinkle of sea salt or fleur de sel. (Pictured on page 121)

WHAT YOU NEED

1   8-ounce package pecan halves, toasted
1   14-ounce package vanilla caramels, unwrapped
1   tablespoon milk
1   12-ounce package dark chocolate pieces
     Coarse sea salt or fleur de sel (optional)

WHAT YOU DO

1. Line a baking sheet or tray with foil or parchment paper; grease the foil or parchment. For each cluster, arrange 5 pecan halves in a single layer close together.
2. In a small heavy saucepan combine caramels and milk. Heat and stir over medium-low heat until caramels melt and mixture is smooth. Spoon some of the caramel mixture over each cluster of pecans. Let stand about 30 minutes or until firm.
3. In a medium heavy saucepan heat and stir dark chocolate pieces over low heat until chocolate melts and is smooth. Spoon melted chocolate over each cluster, gently spreading to the edges. If desired, sprinkle with coarse salt. Let clusters stand about 30 minutes or until set. Place clusters in tin; close tin. Makes 20 to 24 clusters.
To Make Ahead: Layer clusters between sheets of waxed paper in an airtight container; cover. Store in the refrigerator for up to 1 week.

HOW TO MAKE THIS FOOD GIFT

Use masking tape (A) to create stripes on a tin with a windowed lid (B). Cover window with tape. Paint the surface of tin and lid with green paint (C); let dry. Remove tape. Affix pieces of washi tape on white scrapbooking paper (D), folding tape over edges. Cut out triangle shapes. Thread triangles together using kitchen twine (E); wrap around tin.

Hazelnut Rocky Road Brownie Mix

This shelf-stable gift provides treats weeks down the road from the holidays, when the cookie platters have long been empty.

WHAT YOU NEED

1¼ cups granulated sugar
⅔   cup unsweetened cocoa powder
2   ounces milk or dark chocolate, chopped (optional)
1   cup all-purpose flour
¼   teaspoon baking soda
⅛   teaspoon salt
¼   cup chopped toasted hazelnuts
⅓   cup tiny marshmallows

WHAT YOU DO

In a 1-quart jar layer sugar, cocoa powder, and chopped chocolate (if using). In a small bowl stir together flour, baking soda, and salt. Spoon over chocolate in jar. Top with hazelnuts and marshmallows; fasten lid. Include directions for making brownies with gift. Makes 16 brownies.
To Make Brownies: Preheat oven to 325°F. Line a 9×9×2-inch baking pan with foil, extending foil over the edges of the pan. Grease the foil; set pan aside. In a large bowl whisk together ⅔ cup melted butter and 3 eggs until well combined. Add contents of jar to butter mixture; stir until well combined. Spread batter evenly in prepared pan. Bake for 35 minutes. (Moist crumbs will remain attached to wooden toothpick inserted near center of brownies.) Cool brownies in pan on a wire rack. Use foil to lift uncut brownies out of pan. Place on cutting board. Cut into bars.
To Make Ahead: Store jar of mix in a cool, dry place for up to 1 month.

HOW TO MAKE THIS FOOD GIFT

Apply velvet poinsettia stickers (A) to a quart jar (B). Glue a vintage foil flower (C) to a paper tag that contains the recipe (D). Affix a large button (E) to center of flower with glue. Glue tag to lid.

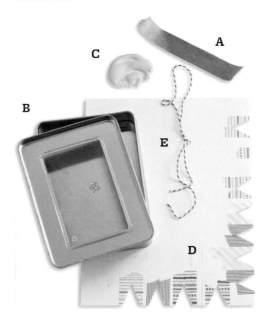

Gingerbread scones

Gingerbread Scones

These tender scones are flavored with cinnamon, molasses, and two kinds of ginger—both ground and crystallized.

WHAT YOU NEED

- 1   cup all-purpose flour
- 1   cup whole wheat flour
- ⅓   cup packed brown sugar
- 2   teaspoons baking powder
- ¾   teaspoon ground ginger
- ½   teaspoon kosher salt
- ½   teaspoon ground cinnamon
- ¼   teaspoon baking soda
- ¼   cup cold butter, cut up
- ½   cup dried currants or raisins
- 1   tablespoon finely chopped crystallized ginger
- 1   egg, lightly beaten
- ½   cup whipping cream
- ¼   cup mild-flavor molasses
- 1   egg white, lightly beaten
- ½   teaspoon water
-      Coarse sugar (optional)

WHAT YOU DO

1. Preheat oven to 375°F. In a large bowl combine all-purpose flour, whole wheat flour, brown sugar, baking powder, ground ginger, salt, cinnamon, and baking soda. Using a pastry blender, cut in butter until mixture resembles coarse crumbs. Stir in the currants and crystallized ginger. Make a well in the center of the flour mixture; set aside.

2. In a small bowl stir together the egg, the whipping cream, and molasses. Add egg mixture all at once to flour mixture. Using a fork, stir just until moistened.

3. Turn dough out onto a lightly floured surface. Knead dough by folding and gently pressing it for 10 to 12 strokes or until dough is nearly smooth. Divide dough in half. Pat or lightly roll each dough half into a 5- to 5½-inch circle that is ¾ inch thick. Cut each circle into six wedges. Place wedges about 2 inches apart on a large ungreased baking sheet. In a small bowl combine egg white and the water. Brush wedges with egg white mixture and, if desired, sprinkle with coarse sugar.

4. Bake for 12 to 15 minutes or until a wooden toothpick inserted into a crack in top of scones comes out clean. Transfer to a wire rack. Serve warm or let cool. Place cooled scones in tin; cover tin. Include directions for reheating scones. Makes 12 scones.

To Reheat Scones: Wrap scones in foil. Heat in a 350°F oven for 12 to 15 minutes or until heated through.

To Make Ahead: Wrap cooled scones in a single layer in foil; place in a freezer bag and seal bag. Freeze for up to 1 month.

HOW TO MAKE THIS FOOD GIFT

Cut several sets of three concentric circles out of red felt (A) with the largest about 2½ inches and the smallest about 1¼ inches. Stack each set of circles and poke a hole through the middle of the three layers. Push a decorative brad (B) through each set. Make about five cuts through layers to the center, then cut corners to shape the flower petals. Arrange flowers in a clustered, meandering line across top of a round white tin (C) and trailing onto the sides. Wrap with pink velvet ribbon (D). Download a gift tag (E) from BHG.com/FGGiftTags and attach tag to the top of the tin.

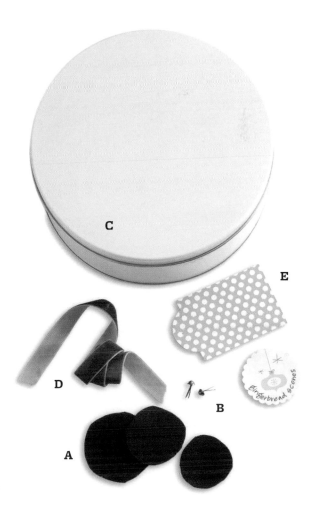

Sugar Cookie Cutouts

These classic cookies are so versatile. Cut them into any shape you like and decorate them in any color scheme that strikes your fancy.

WHAT YOU NEED
⅔ cup butter, softened
¾ cup granulated sugar
1 teaspoon baking powder
¼ teaspoon salt
1 egg
1 tablespoon milk
1 teaspoon vanilla
2 cups all-purpose flour
1 recipe Powdered Sugar Icing (optional)

WHAT YOU DO
1. In a large mixing bowl beat butter on medium to high speed for 30 seconds. Add granulated sugar, baking powder, and salt. Beat until combined, scraping sides of bowl occasionally. Beat in egg, milk, and vanilla until combined. Beat in as much of the flour as you can with the mixer. Stir in any remaining flour. Divide dough in half. Cover and chill dough about 30 minutes or until easy to handle.
2. Preheat oven to 375°F. On a floured surface, roll half the dough at a time to ⅛- to ¼-inch thickness. Using a 2½-inch cookie cutter, cut into desired shapes. Place 1 inch apart on ungreased cookie sheets.
3. Bake for 7 to 10 minutes or until edges are firm and bottoms are very light brown. Transfer cookies to wire racks and let cool. If desired, frost with Powdered Sugar Icing. Makes 36 to 48 cookies.

HOW TO MAKE THIS FOOD GIFT
Allow icing to dry completely before packaging. To create gift box, cut squares of parchment paper with pinking shears. Layer cookies between layers of parchment paper in a decorative box. Tie box with a decorative ribbon.

Powdered Sugar Icing

Make this icing on the thinner side for the base colors so that it washes over the cookie and creates a smooth surface. Make the icing thicker for the colors you pipe to create decorative details.

WHAT YOU NEED
4 cups powdered sugar
1 teaspoon vanilla
4 tablespoons milk
  Milk

WHAT YOU DO
In a large bowl combine powdered sugar, vanilla, and 4 tablespoons milk. Stir in additional milk, 1 teaspoon at a time, until icing reaches desired consistency. Makes 1 cup.

Wasabi Almonds and Popcorn

This savory snack is super-quick to make. For maximum freshness, give it away the day it's made.

WHAT YOU NEED
6	cups air-popped popcorn (unsalted)
4	ounces wasabi- and soy-flavor whole almonds, coarsely chopped
1	cup sesame sticks or sesame oat bran sticks
2	tablespoons butter
¼	teaspoon garlic powder
¼	teaspoon onion powder
¼	teaspoon curry powder (optional)

WHAT YOU DO
In a large bowl combine popcorn, almonds, and sesame sticks. In a 1-cup microwave-safe glass measure, microwave butter on high about 30 seconds or until butter melts. Stir in garlic powder, onion powder, and curry powder (if using). Drizzle butter mixture over popcorn mixture; toss well to coat. Place popcorn mixture in tin; close tin. Makes 8 cups.

To Make Ahead: Place popcorn mixture in a resealable plastic bag or airtight container; seal bag or cover. Store at room temperature for up to 1 day.

HOW TO MAKE THIS FOOD GIFT
Apply washi tapes (A) across the lids of two tins (B), creating stripes. Cut stocking shapes and stocking tops from four colored felts (C). Using fabric glue, affix tops to stocking shapes. Stitch a snowflake with white thread into one of the stockings. Thread them onto twine or colored string (D) and wrap them around the tins. Attach a gift tag (E) from the downloadable patterns at BHG.com/FGGiftTags

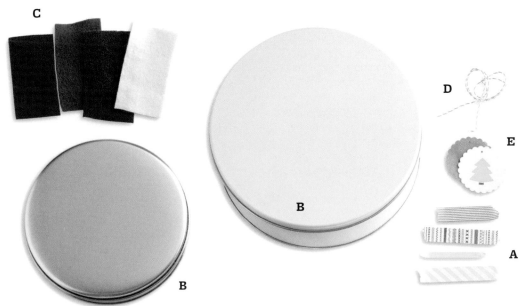

Roasted Pepper Hummus

This popular dip makes a great hostess gift. It's always a welcome addition to any appetizer spread.

WHAT YOU NEED
- 2   red sweet peppers*
- 4   cloves garlic, unpeeled*
- 1   15-ounce can garbanzo beans (chickpeas), rinsed and drained
- ¼   cup sliced green onions (2)
- ¼   cup tahini (sesame seed paste)
- 2   tablespoons lemon juice
- ½   teaspoon salt
- ¼   teaspoon paprika
-      Dash crushed red pepper (optional)
- ⅓   cup olive oil
- 2   to 3 teaspoons olive oil (optional)
- 2   tablespoons pine nuts, toasted (optional)
- 1   tablespoon snipped fresh Italian (flat-leaf) parsley (optional)
-      Toasted pita wedges

WHAT YOU DO
1. Preheat oven to 425°F. Cut sweet peppers in half lengthwise; remove stems, seeds, and membranes. Place pepper halves, cut sides down, on a foil-lined baking sheet. Arrange unpeeled garlic around peppers. Roast for 20 to 25 minutes or until peppers are charred and tender. Bring foil up around peppers and garlic and fold edges together to enclose. Let stand about 15 minutes or until cool enough to handle. Using a sharp knife, loosen edges of pepper skins; gently pull off skins in strips and discard. Peel garlic.

2. In a blender or food processor combine roasted peppers and garlic, garbanzo beans, green onions, tahini, lemon juice, salt, paprika, and crushed red pepper (if using). Cover and blend or process until smooth, scraping sides of container as necessary. With the machine running, add ⅓ cup oil in a slow, steady stream until combined.

3. Transfer hummus to a gift container. If desired, drizzle with 2 to 3 teaspoons oil and sprinkle with pine nuts and/ or parsley; cover. Include pita wedges with gift. Makes 3 cups.

*Tip: To save time, use ¾ cup bottled roasted red sweet peppers and 2 teaspoons bottled minced roasted garlic in place of the fresh peppers and garlic.

To Make Ahead: Transfer hummus to an airtight container; cover. Store in the refrigerator for up to 3 days.

HOW TO MAKE THIS FOOD GIFT
Reuse a plastic container with a lid (A) and lightly coat the outside of the container with frosted spray paint; let dry. Attach self-adhesive decorative letters (B) to spell JOY to the outside of the container. Make a paper cone out of white bakery paper (C) and fill with pita wedges. Wrap a gold ribbon (D) around the container and tie.

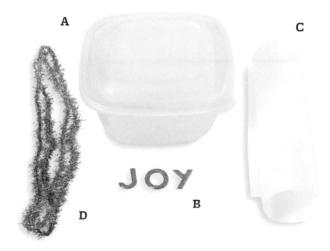

Sweet and Smoky Nuts

These salty, sweet, and smoky nuts are great with a glass of wine or holiday punch. (Pictured on page 120)

WHAT YOU NEED

1 egg white
1 cup dry roasted peanuts
1 cup whole almonds or hazelnuts (filberts)
1 cup pecan or walnut halves
⅓ cup packed brown sugar
1½ teaspoons smoked paprika
1 teaspoon kosher salt
¼ teaspoon ground cinnamon
¼ teaspoon ground allspice

WHAT YOU DO

1. Preheat oven to 350°F. Line a 15×10×1-inch baking pan with foil or parchment paper. Set aside.
2. In a large bowl whisk egg white until foamy. Add peanuts, almonds, and pecans; toss gently to coat. Stir in brown sugar, paprika, salt, cinnamon, and allspice. Spread nuts in an even layer in the prepared baking pan.
3. Bake for 25 to 30 minutes or until nuts are toasted and appear dry, stirring twice. Remove from oven and stir again. Cool completely in baking pan. Break up any large clusters. Makes 4 cups.
To Make Ahead: Store nuts in an airtight container at room temperature for up to 2 weeks.

HOW TO MAKE THIS FOOD GIFT

Using a crafts knife, cut the top out of the lid of a takeout soup container (A). Cut out a circle of patterned acetate scrapbooking paper (B) and adhere it to the inside of the lid using hot glue. Place the lid on the container. Tie a ribbon (C) around the container and attach a gift tag (D) and an adornment.

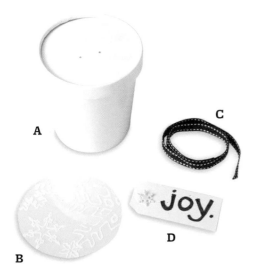

Marinated Feta and Olives

Start marinating in the morning, and this Mediterranean-style appetizer will be ready to give as a gift that evening.

WHAT YOU NEED

16 ounces feta cheese, cut into ½-inch cubes
1 cup pitted Kalamata olives
1 cup pitted green olives
½ cup bottled roasted red sweet peppers, cut into strips
1 red onion, cut into thin wedges
½ cup olive oil
½ cup white or red balsamic vinegar
4 cloves garlic, minced
1 tablespoon snipped fresh thyme
2 teaspoons snipped fresh oregano
½ teaspoon cracked black pepper

WHAT YOU DO

1. In a large glass or stainless-steel bowl combine cheese cubes, Kalamata olives, green olives, sweet pepper strips, and onion.
2. In a screw-top jar combine oil, vinegar, garlic, thyme, oregano, and black pepper. Cover and shake well. Pour over olive mixture; toss gently to coat.
3. Cover and marinate in the refrigerator for 4 to 6 hours. Spoon into decorative jars or glasses; cover. Makes 5 cups.
To Make Ahead: Store olive mixture in the refrigerator for up to 2 days.

HOW TO MAKE THIS FOOD GIFT

On a piece of decorative scrapbooking paper (A), trace disk lid and cut out. Glue paper circle to top of lid (B). Cut a strip of kraft paper (C) to match width of screw band and glue to band. Near bottom of glass jar (D), wrap lacy trim (E) around jar and glue. Make a wide kraft paper band (F) for jar. Glue a strip of creamy white paper (G) to paper band. Top with a piece of narrow lacy trim (H) and glue. Overlap top of trim on the jar with the band and glue. Glue paper dots (I) to ends of wooden toothpicks (J). Weave picks into trim.

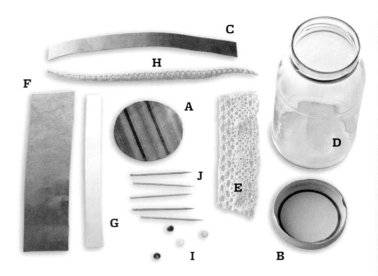

Making
Spirits Bright

Let bold colors and graphic patterns bring
the happy into your holiday this year.

Pretty Patterned Stockings

Chevron and polka-dot patterns combine with buttons and pinked edges to create oh-so-fun stockings for Santa to fill this year.

WHAT YOU NEED

Pencil • ½ yard body stocking fabric • ½ yard lining fabric • ¼ yard contrast fabric for cuffs, toe, and heel • ¼ yard white felt • 2⅓×7-inch strip of fabric for hanging loop • Lightweight interfacing • Scissors • Pinking shears • Matching sewing thread • Buttons

WHAT YOU DO

1. Enlarge stocking patterns, right, reversing one of the shapes, and cut out. Trace around patterns onto appropriate fabrics and cut out. Also cut toe, heel, and cuff pieces from felt. Set cuff pieces aside.

2. Layer print fabric and felt for toe and heel pieces. Baste around edges and pink edges. Position on stocking front and back and topstitch in place.

3. Stitch body stocking front and back pieces with right sides together, leaving top edge open, using ¼-inch seam. Clip curves. Turn right side out.

4. Stitch lining pieces with right sides together, using ⅜-inch seam. Trim the seam close to stitching to reduce bulk in stocking. Turn in long edges of loop, bringing long edges to center. Fold in half and stitch close to long open edge. Insert lining inside turned stocking, keeping top straight edges even. Fold loop in half and baste to upper back edge of stocking on lining side.

5. Layer cuff pieces with felt. Baste in place and pink edges. Stitch short ends of cuff together with right sides together. Turn. Pin right side of cuff to wrong side of stocking. Stitch. Turn cuff to outside. Press stocking body lightly.

6. Sew buttons to cuff where desired.

Pretty Patterned Stockings Cuff

Enlarge 300%

Fold

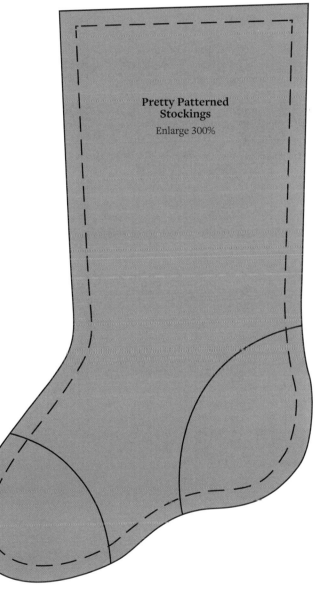

Pretty Patterned Stockings

Enlarge 300%

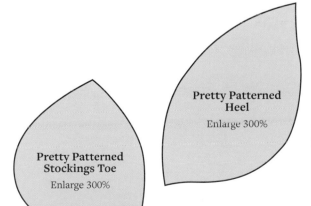

Pretty Patterned Heel

Enlarge 300%

Pretty Patterned Stockings Toe

Enlarge 300%

Tiny buttons form a little Christmas tree on a purchased pillow that reveals favorite Christmas songs.

Merry Christmas Pillows

Personalize purchased pillows with your own messages and sweet little embellishments.

WHAT YOU NEED
Purchased pillows with stripes or chevron design • Practice paper • Permanent fine-tip marker • Small buttons • Scraps of felt • Thread • Needle • Scissors

WHAT YOU DO
1. Plan the pillow design. Practice writing the desired words on paper first.
2. Write the words on the pillow using the fine-tip permanent marker.
3. Group buttons to form a tree shape or add felt holly leaves around buttons to embellish, sewing the buttons on with thread.

Polka-Dot Owl Garland

Quickly crafted from fabric and felt, these tiny owls add a fresh perspective swinging from a strip of double-fold bias tape.

WHAT YOU NEED

Transfer paper • ⅛ yard each of red and green polka-dot fabrics • Scraps of white, green, and gold felt • Eyelet hole punch and eyelet hammer • 2 yards of green ⅜-inch-wide satin ribbon • Polyester fiberfill • Fabric glue • 2 yards ecru 1-inch-wide double-fold bias tape • Red sewing thread

WHAT YOU DO

1. Trace patterns, below, onto tracing paper. Using transfer paper, transfer patterns onto cardboard for templates. Cut out templates.
2. Trace six owl bodies onto the wrong side of the red polka-dot fabric and eight bodies onto the wrong side of the green polka-dot fabric, leaving at least ½ inch between shapes for seam allowances. Cut out bodies, adding ¼-inch seam allowances.
3. Trace 14 eyes onto white felt; cut out. Using eyelet hole punch and eyelet hammer, punch 14 pupils from green felt. Cut seven beaks from gold felt.
4. Cut two 17-inch lengths of green satin ribbon for garland ties. From remaining ribbon, cut seven 5-inch-long pieces of ribbon.
5. For each owl, place two green (or red) bodies with right sides together. Slip a length of ribbon between the bodies, matching one ribbon end to the center top of the body. Sew around body, leaving an opening at the bottom for stuffing. Turn right side out and stuff with fiberfill. Sew opening closed. Glue pupils to eyes. Glue eyes and beak in place on each owl.
6. Fold one ribbon garland tie in half. Slip folded end into short end of bias tape; pin in place. Repeat with other ribbon tie at opposite end. Place owls along bias tape, pinning ribbon ends inside the tape. Using red sewing thread, topstitch around the bias tape, catching ribbons as you sew.

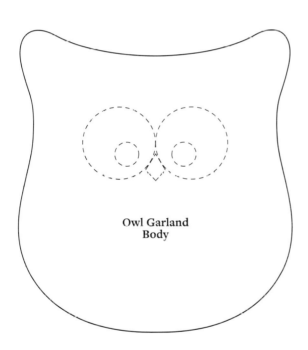

Owl Garland Body

Owl Garland Eye

A Touch of Lime

Christmas red with a touch of lime makes spirits bright. Purchased stockings are filled with packages wrapped in red and lime green. On the mantel, fabric doilies shaped into trees and spray-painted bright red look holiday-hip. The potted tree brims with character thanks to hand-crafted ornaments. The touch-of-lime paper wreath adds the perfect holiday hue.

Red Doily Tree

Pretty doilies are the secret to making these clever cutwork-looking trees.

WHAT YOU NEED

Cardstock • Plastic-foam cone, such as Styrofoam (14-inch, 18-inch, and 20-inch cones) • Straight pins • Plastic wrap • Stiffening glue, such as Aleene's Fabric Stiffener & Draping Liquid • Disposable foam plates • Assorted lace doilies • Thin, flexible ruler • Sponge brush • Red spray paint, such as Krylon Short Cuts in Red Pepper • Hot-glue gun and glue sticks

WHAT YOU DO

1. Wrap cardstock around the plastic-foam cone, forming a point at the top. Push pins through the overlaps to hold the cardstock in place. Trim the paper flush with the base of the cone. Wrap the paper-covered cone with plastic wrap, taping the edges down if necessary.

2. Pour stiffening glue onto a disposable plate, making a puddle slightly larger than the doily. Place the doily on the glue to coat one side; flip the doily and coat the other side. Position the glue-covered doily on the cone, pinning to hold it in place. Coat and adhere another doily in the same manner, slightly overlapping the edges of the first doily. Continue adding doilies until the cone is covered. Wrap doilies near the base slightly underneath the cone; pin to the bottom. Let dry overnight.

3. Choose a doily that is slightly larger than the base of the cone. Coat both sides of the doily with glue and let it dry flat on a disposable plate. Set aside.

4. Remove pins from the cone. Gently bend back the doilies wrapped under the cone. Run the ruler between the doilies and the cone to loosen them. Remove the ruler. Gently twist and pull the cone to remove it from inside the doilies. The doily tree should now stand on its own. If it needs to be stiffer, place it back onto the plastic-wrapped cone. Reapply stiffening glue to the outside of the doilies with a sponge brush and let dry.

5. When satisfied with the stiffness of the doily tree, place it back on the plastic-wrapped cone. Spray-paint the doilies red, using short bursts and working in a well-ventilated area. Let dry. Spray-paint the flat doily. When all the doilies are dry, remove the doily tree from the plastic-wrapped cone as before. Hot-glue the flat doily to the bottom of the doily tree; trim the edges of the flat doily flush with the base of the doily tree.

Newspaper-Petal Wreath

Who would guess that a daily newspaper could become an elegant wreath?

WHAT YOU NEED

½-inch-diameter PEX pipe • ½-inch foam pipe insulation • ⁷⁄₁₆-inch Wooden dowel • Natural muslin strips • Hot-glue gun and glue sticks • Newspaper • Lime green paint

WHAT YOU DO

1. Wrap 60-inch length of pipe with insulation tubing. To form a circle shape, insert the dowel at each end to connect, securing with tape if desired. Wrap muslin strips around the tube, gluing the ends.

2. Paint eight newspaper sheets, front and back; let dry. Fold each sheet into 4-inch strips. Enlarge the petal pattern, below, and cut out. Using the pattern, cut the strips to get four petals. Repeat for approximately 240 petals. Fold several petals in half lengthwise and glue in place at the base. Glue the leaves on the outside and inside edges of the wreath. Roll the base corners of several petals toward the center and glue in place on the petal base. Fill the middle of the wreath with rolled petals, leaving space for the newspaper flowers.

3. To create the flowers, cut 6-inch strips of newspaper. Glue ends together, forming a 45-inch long strip. Fold strip lengthwise twice, so only folded edges are visible. Tightly roll the strip, holding in place with glue. Occasionally twist the strip, then continue to roll the newspaper. When you achieve the size of flower you desire, glue the end on the back of the flower and trim excess paper. Repeat instructions for the remaining flowers. Paint the flowers and let dry. Glue in place on the wreath.

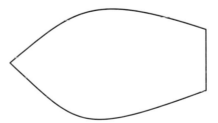

Newspaper-Petal Wreath Petal

Enlarge 200%

SATIN RIBBON ROSE

RING THE BELL

SHEET MUSIC ROSE

Satin Ribbon Rose

Melted edges on the ribbon circles create the fluttery petals.

WHAT YOU NEED

Red single-face satin ribbon (2- and 3-inches wide) • Lime green single-face satin ribbon (1½ inches wide) • Votive candle and matches • Sewing needle and sewing thread to match ribbon • Faux gems, beads, or old costume jewelry • Hot-glue gun and glue sticks

WHAT YOU DO

1. For each flower, cut four circles of graduated sizes from red satin ribbon. **Note:** The circles can be roughly cut; just be sure to have rounded corners. Before curling, snip small slits around the circle's edge if desired. Light the candle. Hold each circle close to the flame (do not touch it!) until the ribbon starts to melt and curl in.
2. Stack the circles; when satisfied with the look, sew the circles together at the bottom. Knot the thread at the back.
3. For each flower, cut a 1½- to 2-inch length of lime green ribbon. Hold one end over the votive flame until it curls unto a leaf shape. Hot-glue the leaf to the bottom of the rose so the point is visible.
4. Hot-glue a gem or other bauble to the center of the rose. If you like, sew a loop of thread at the center back of the flower to use as a hanging loop.

Ring the Bell

Honeycomb tissue paper gives the bell its 3-D fluff.

WHAT YOU NEED

Honeycomb ornament bell pattern • Honeycomb tissue pad: white (available at crafts supply stores and online) • Crafts glue • ¾-inch diameter wooden bead with center hole • White embroidery floss

WHAT YOU DO

1. Using the honeycomb ornament bell pattern, right, trace the half-bell shape onto the honeycomb crafts paper, aligning the straight edge of the pattern along the glue line of the honeycomb paper. Cut out the shape.

2. Unfold the accordionlike tissue paper. Glue the two end pieces together to form a bell. Use a paper clip to hold the bell together until the glue dries. Thread embroidery floss through the wooden bead, knotting one end. With the remaining floss, thread through the bell center and tie for a hanging loop.

Sheet Music Rose

Old sheet music sings a new tune when cut into a spiral and coiled into a rose.

WHAT YOU NEED

Sheet music pages • Crafts glue • Red seed bead

WHAT YOU DO

1. Cut an irregular circular shape, about 9 inches in diameter, from sheet music. Referring to the diagram, below, cut a spiral into the shape in a continuous coil about ¾ inch wide. The cutting does not need to be perfect. Roll the spiral into a flower shape and glue to secure.
2. Cut a small piece of sheet music slightly smaller than the flower for a base. Glue the bottom of the flower to the base. Glue the red bead to the center of the flower.

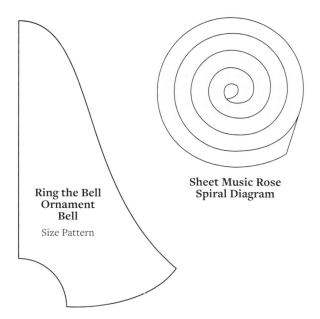

Ring the Bell Ornament Bell

Size Pattern

Sheet Music Rose Spiral Diagram

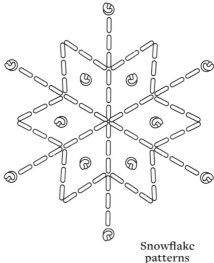

Snowflake
patterns

Embroidered Ease

*Embroidery hoops that are on-trend as art make nifty
ornaments. This snowflake design is stitched in minutes.*

WHAT YOU NEED
• 3- or 4-inch-diameter wooden embroidery hoops
• 7-inch square lime green cotton fabric • White
embroidery needle and floss • 7-inch square thin white
cotton batting • Sewing needle and sewing thread

WHAT YOU DO
1. Trace or photocopy the desired snowflake, above right,
enlarging if needed to fit your embroidery hoops. Place the
fabric in the embroidery hoop. Using a pencil, trace the
snowflake onto the fabric square.
2. For either pattern, use the embroidery needle and six
strands of white embroidery floss to backstitch the
straight snowflake lines; use two strands to stitch

double-wrapped French knots on the dots. (For Stitch
Diagrams, see page 160.) After embroidering the
snowflake, remove the fabric from the hoop.
3. Using a warm iron, gently press fabric around the
stitching. Lay the completed embroidery on top of the
cotton batting. Insert embroidery and batting into the
hoop. Adjust the fabrics to center the designs. Tighten
each hoop screw to hold everything in place. Trim the
batting flush with the back hoop edges. Trim the
embroidered fabric edges approximately 2 inches from the
hoop edges.
4. Thread a needle with sewing thread and knot the ends.
Sew a long running stitch around the edges of the excess
fabric at the back of the hoop, folding it at intervals. Pull
the ends of the thread to gather the fabric; tie off the
thread ends.

Little Felt Boxes

Squares of Christmas-color felt are sewn seam-side out to create sweet little boxes that hold holiday goodies.

WHAT YOU NEED

For the Red Box:
Red felt: Four 4×3-inch pieces (sides) • One 4×4-inch piece (bottom)
White felt: Four 4×3-inch pieces (sides)

For the Green Box:
Green felt: Four 4×5-inch pieces (sides) • One 4×4-inch piece (bottom)
White felt: Four 4×5-inch pieces (sides)

For both boxes:
⅛-inch and 16-inch hole punch • Spray glue • Embroidery floss • Sewing machine (optional)

WHAT YOU DO

1. Using hole punches, punch the design on the side pieces using the templates, below. Or create your own design.
Tip: Place a piece of masking tape on the felt and draw on the masking tape. It will help stabilize the felt as you punch it.
2. Attach four white side pieces to four red side pieces with spray glue. Placing white sides together, stitch down the side allowing for a ¼-inch seam allowance. **Note:** This can be hand-stitched if you don't have a sewing machine.
3. Attach the bottom of the box with embroidery floss using a whip stitch.

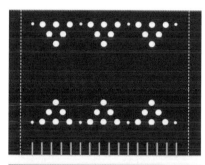

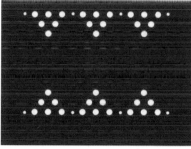

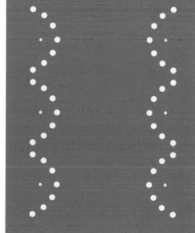

● ⅛-inch circle punch
• 1/16-inch circle punch

Felt Birdie Stocking

This elegant stocking is surprisingly easy to stitch together. Play with color and positioning of the wing and leaf pieces to alter your design or add simple embellishments if you like. (See page 135 for alternative color combinations.)

WHAT YOU NEED

Tracing paper • Pencil • Nonwoven felt such as National Nonwovens 30% Woolfelt: two shades of green: ½ yard Light Green; ½ yard Dark Green; ¼ yard *each* of White, Stonefield and Red • 2 Black glass beads • Red and green thread • Scissors • Sewing machine • Sewing needles • Straight pins

WHAT YOU DO

1. Enlarge and trace the patterns, below. Add seam allowance to stocking but not to the cuffs and embellishments. Cut the following pieces out of felt: For one stocking: two base pieces out of the Light Green, two Stonefield Cuffs, two 6×¾-inch hanging strips one Green and one Stonefield, one red bird body and wing, two large leaves and four small leaves out of White felt.

2. Arrange and stitch the leaves and bird pieces to the front stocking base. Position the pieces 1½ inches down from the top and 1 inch in from either side. You can alter the design by changing the wing position and leaf placement. Once you're pleased with the arrangement, pin the pieces in place. Thread the machine with green thread and make a single seam down the center of each leaf. Switch to red thread to stitch the bird in place. Set the wing aside and encircle the bird's body with a single seam that contours the outside edge. Replace the wing and make

a second seam around the wing edge. Hand-stitch the bead eye to the bird's head.

3. Stack the stocking bases together, right side facing out. Place the cuff pieces between the stockings. The cuffs should extend 1 inch beyond the stocking tops. Line up the cuff zig zags, then carefully keep them in position while pinning a cuff to the top of each stocking base. Separate the stockings and machine stitch the cuffs in place with green thread. Make a single seam ¼ inch down from the top stocking edge.

4. Stitch hanging strips together and hand-sew them to the finished stocking. Stack and pin the Light Green and Stonefield hanging strips together. Machine-stitch down either side of the strips with green thread. Fold the hanging strip in half and then sew it inside the top right hand corner of the stocking. Stitch the hanging strips ends to the top edge of the stocking. Make a series of small stitches that connect through all the felt layers, making sure the hanging strip is securely connected to both the cuff and stocking.

5. Embellish stocking front with various sizes of beads and small feathers, if desired.

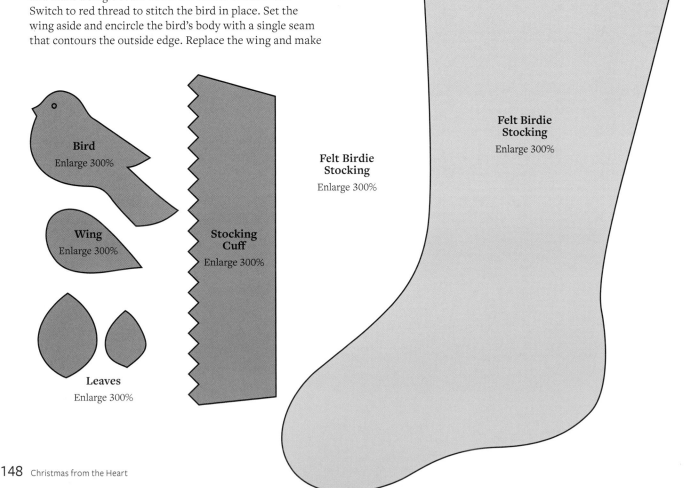

Bird
Enlarge 300%

Wing
Enlarge 300%

Leaves
Enlarge 300%

Stocking Cuff
Enlarge 300%

Felt Birdie Stocking
Enlarge 300%

Felt Birdie Stocking
Enlarge 300%

Merry in Minutes

Create simple yet stunning decorations and crafts for your
holiday home—just in the nick of time.

Simple Reflections

Purchased mirrors take on a new look when they are embellished with colorful trims.

WHAT YOU NEED
Purchased circle mirrors • Pom-pom by the yard to fit around the mirror edge • Crafts glue • Felt balls in desired colors • Adhesive-back jewels

WHAT YOU DO
1. Plan the placement of the pom-poms, felt balls, and adhesive jewels.
2. Use crafts glue to glue the pom-pom yardage or felt balls to the mirror edge. Let dry. Adhere the jewels to the mirror edge using the adhesive backing.

Make a big statement with little projects that you create using find-around-the-house items. Embellish them with scraps of small-print papers, adhesive jewels, and stickers.

Clever Christmas Clips

Colorful binder clips can be transformed into place cards, money gift holders, or bag toppers with bits of paper and small stickers.

WHAT YOU NEED

Red or green large binder clips • Small stickers and borders • Small-print scrapbook paper • Glue stick • Pencil • Ruler • Scissors

WHAT YOU DO

1. Measure the size of the clip and cut scrapbook paper to fit. Glue in place.
2. Decorate the paper with small stickers and bits of paper. Use as desired.

Holiday Clothespin Helpers

Scraps of paper and sparking jewels turn ho-hum clothespins into holiday helpers.

WHAT YOU NEED

Wood snap-style clothespins • Scraps of tiny-print scrapbook paper • Glue stick • Adhesive-back jewels • Ruler • Pencil

WHAT YOU DO

1. Measure the clothespin and cut the scrapbook paper to fit. Glue in place.
2. Add a jewel to the top of the clothespin.

Snow-Touched Candles

Create candles that shimmer with the season by using a most unexpected dash of salt.

WHAT YOU NEED
Purchased candles in desired color • Crafts glue •
2 Paintbrushes • Epsom salt • Cake pan or dish

WHAT YOU DO
1. Be sure the candles are clean and dry. Pour the salt into the pan so it is 2 inches thick.
2. Plan the design. Paint the design on the candle using crafts glue. Roll the candle in the salt. Use the dry paintbrush to remove any unwanted salt. Let dry.

Never leave a burning candle unattended.

Bells Under Glass

Jingle all the way with bells tucked under a dome of glass.

WHAT YOU NEED
Glass compote with dome lid (available at crafts stores) • Jingle bells in desired colors

WHAT YOU DO
1. Be sure the glass is clean and dry.
2. Turn the dome upside down and fill with jingle bells. Put the compote bottom over the bells in the top and turn right side up.

Choose letter stickers or stamps to spell out your Christmas greeting this year. Display them on a clever candle centerpiece or tucked away on a favorite bookshelf.

Merry Reading

Vintage books spell out holiday cheer with simple stamped letters and a few shiny baubles.

WHAT YOU NEED

Castaway vintage books with white or cream pages • Large alphabet stamps • Black stamp pad • Burlap ribbon • Twine • Small vintage ornaments

WHAT YOU DO

1. Choose the word to be stamped on the book page ends. Use the alphabet stamps and stamp pad to stamp one letter on each book. Let dry.
2. Stack the books together to spell the word. Wrap the burlap around the books and then wrap the twine around the burlap. Tie to secure. Thread the ornaments on another piece of twine and tie around the twine and burlap adding a bow in the front.

Noel Candle

Alphabet stickers make it easy to spell out a message for your holiday guests.

WHAT YOU NEED

Square-shape glass container • Alphabet stickers • Fresh cranberries • Red taper candle

WHAT YOU DO

1. Be sure the container is clean and dry. Adhere the stickers to one of the sides of the container to spell the desired words.
2. Place the candle in the center of the container. Fill the container with cranberries.

Never leave a burning candle unattended.

Stitch Diagrams

Backstitch

Chain Stitch

French Knot

Running Stitch

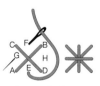

Star Stitch

Stem Stitch

Whip Stitch

Cross Stitch

Straight Stitch

Fern Stitch

Blanket Stitch

Index

Craft Designers

Judy Bailey • Heidi Boyd • Sonja Carmon • Laura Collins • Carol Field Dahlstrom • Pam Koelling • Katie LaPorte • Janet Pittman • Margaret Sindelar • Jan Teymeyer

Sources

Beads—thebeadmonkey.com
Felt—National Nonwovens Woolfelt.com
Paint—deltacreative.com, plaidonline.com
General Crafting Supplies—hobbylobby.com, michaels.com
Paper/Scrapbooking Supplies americancrafts.com, bazzillbasics.com
Paper tape/ribbon—cutetape.com